Dr. Marty Seldman's

SUPER SELLING

THROUGH

SELF-TALK

The Ultimate Edge in Sales Success

PRICE STERN SLOAN, INC.
Los Angeles, California

Published by Price Stern Sloan, Inc.
310 N. La Cienega Blvd.
Los Angeles, CA 90048

Printed in U.S.A.
9 8 7 6 5 4 3 2 1

Library of Congress Cataloging-in-Publication Data

Seldman, Marty.
  Super selling through self-talk.
  Rev. ed. of: Self-talk. c1986.
  Bibliography: p.
  1. Selling. I. Seldman, Marty. Self-talk.
I. Title.
HF5438.25.S4375   1988   658.8'5   87-22581

ISBN 0-89586-674-9 (pbk.)

To the memory of my grandparents–

Annie, Sadie, Harry, and Raphael–

for their courage and sacrifice

ACKNOWLEDGMENTS

Sandy Smith has often been my cotrainer in self-talk and sales seminars, and he contributed greatly to the development of this book. I'm also grateful to Larry Wilson for the opportunity to work with and learn from him and Dr. Maxie Maultsby.

Karen Feinberg edited my work and often guided me in the writing and publishing process. Working with her was very rewarding.

Many of my friends and associates who are sales professionals helped shape my efforts by reading and critiquing early drafts. I owe a special debt to Bob and Dot Bolton and Rick Brandon for their extensive and detailed suggestions.

In addition I sincerely thank: Mark Bernardi, Diane Blecha, Betsey Bolton, Dave Bosson, Don Bushman, Mary Laura Bushman, Herb Freidman, Rick Farrington, Barry Hupp, Tom Jacoby, Morris Shriftman, Cynthia Vance, and George West.

A special thanks to Bill Byrne for the opportunity to work with him and his sales force during the past eight years.

Finally I'd like to express my appreciation to the salespeople who have taught me directly and through personal example: Terry Schauer, Phil Catanzaro, Paul Carvin, Mickey Howard, Jack Eubank, Steve Whitehurst, Dot Bolton, Gary Greenip, George Van Cott, Paul Kleiber, Roberta Seldman, Ken Oliver, Dave Chapman, and Jay Finley.

Notes on Style

NONSEXIST LANGUAGE

A 1986 survey by the Research Institute of America, Inc., shows that 36.5 percent of the salespeople in the United States are women. I have attempted to reflect this reality by using saleswomen in many of my examples.

FICTITIOUS NAMES

The names of the salespersons, customers, and companies used in sales scenarios are purely fictitious.

CONTENTS

PART III
During the Sale

PART IV
After the Sale

The Sales Challenge

EXERCISES AND ACTIVITIES

FOREWORD

SOONER OR LATER every successful salesperson develops an effective method to sell his or her wares, regardless of the product line—insurance, real estate, securities, computers, and so on. With this in mind, the easiest part about selling should be the actual eyeball-to-eyeball sales presentation.

What separates a top producer from the rest of the pack is the selling that's necessary to convince *you,* the salesperson, that *you can do it!* That doesn't sound too difficult, does it? It isn't—once you know how to do it. This sell-yourself sales presentation is what Dr. Marty Seldman calls Self-Talk, a technique he has researched and mastered. Now he's consulting with leading corporations all over the world and conducting Self-Talk seminars for their salespeople. Self-Talk is the missing ingredient that makes up the difference between mediocrity and big success in the sales field.

Have you ever meet an individual who was billed as one of the top producers in his industry and after you met him, you've wondered, "What does he have that makes him (or her) so successful?" Perhaps you, like I, have met a leading salesperson who didn't fit the mold—he or she wasn't the stereotype. You know, the person with a wonderful gift of gab, great appearance, and plenty of smarts. On the surface, the super sales producer seemed to lack the stuff that you expect to find in a great salesperson.

But what every superstar salesperson *does* have going for him is what this book can bring out in everyone who uses it. Sure, there are many super salespersons who have never heard of Seldman's

Self-Talk concept, but that doesn't mean they aren't out there applying its proven principles every day. Marty Seldman doesn't claim to own a patent on how to reach the top pinnacle of success in your field—but he has developed a workable program that incorporates what all top sales achievers constantly use. Whether they know it or not!

The sad truth is that the vast majority of salespersons simply go through the motions of selling every day; they are drifting and lack direction. They simply aren't using what this book advocates. And that is apparent by their low sales productivity. So, instead of leaving it to chance that *maybe* one day you will stumble across some magic formula that will elevate you into the elite ranks of the top salespeople in your field, you now have the opportunity to do something to make things happen. After all, your future is too important to leave to fate.

Super Selling Through Self-Talk promises to teach you how to make the most important sale of all—the job of selling yourself. Because, once you're sold on you, many other sales will come your way. This is not only an important book for every salesperson to read again and again, it's a way of life to *live* by. Keep this book handy—and refer to it again and again. It will make an important difference.

—Robert L. Shook, Best-selling author of *The Perfect Sales Presentation, The IBM Way* (with Buck Rogers), *The Entrepreneurs,* and many other classic books on salesmanship and business.

INTRODUCTION

Sales Self-Management

The race does not always go to the swift,

The battle does not always go to the strong,

. . . but that's the way to bet!

—Damon Runyon

BUSINESSES MAKE SIZABLE investments in their salespeople. The costs of training, generating leads, maintaining support staff, and phone, mail, and travel expenses add up to a significant wager on your performance. McGraw-Hill's Laboratory of Advertising Performance has found that the 800 largest American companies spend an average of $42,000 on a salesperson before he or she earns a dollar for the company. If you own your own business, even more may be riding on your sales achievements.

This book is designed to give you a winning edge by teaching you how to manage and master your most valuable assets: your attitudes and your emotions. It contains a proven step-by-step program of mental skills and techniques that can put you in charge of yourself at every stage of a sale.

These internal skills are easy to learn, and they can quickly become productive mental habits that you apply automatically while selling. They are the skills that allow you to use to the fullest your knowledge of the product, your social competence, and your sales talent.

Sales Achievement **=** **Acquiring sales skills and product knowledge + Being able to use your skills and knowledge when it counts**

The "Self-Talk" system helps you master the inner game of selling. The goal is to help you:

Build *positive persistence* in generating leads and prospects;

Create an *inner environment* that maximizes the chances for top performance in each sales contact;

Learn rapidly and *improve* from every sales experience;

Develop the *mental toughness* that is necessary for sustained achievement in a sales career.

The Focus Is On You

Most of all, this is a book about you. You work in an outer world of selling that includes your products, services, marketplace, prospects, and customers. As you go through each chapter you will also become more aware of your *inner* environment; the inner thoughts and words that accompany you when you sell. You can discover how you really sell, from the inside out, and then acquire the internal skills that maximize your effectiveness and consistency.

When you complete the activities, charts, and profiles that follow, you will know what your attitudes and feelings are at each stage of the sales process. Then you will discover how the top sales pros talk to themselves and manage their emotions and motivational levels.

You will learn:

Professional sales preparation, including the key skills of *planning, choosing your self-talk, relaxation,* and *mental rehearsal.*

Positive self-motivation, including how to want to do what you don't like to do and eight techniques for *conquering procrastination.*

Self-management, including skills for reducing the three emotions that hurt sales performance the most: FEAR, ANGER, and DISCOURAGEMENT.

The **attitude of a learner,** including the attitudes and skills that enable you to learn rapidly from every sales contact.

This example from real life shows how a saleswoman used some of the "winning edge" skills.

Susan T.—Meeting a Sales Challenge

In 1981 many apartments in the Atlanta area were converted to condominiums. Susan was part of a small sales team that presold the units while they were being renovated. Most of Susan's 31 sales were made to owner-occupants who put 5% down; the rest of the financing was to be provided through the developer.

On the Monday two weeks before the sales were to close, Susan was informed that interest rates had increased and that developer-financed mortgages would have to be 2% higher than the buyers had expected. Each buyer would have to be informed, and would have the right to cancel the sales agreement. Susan was given a week to call her 31 buyers, explain the situation, and try to avoid cancellations.

On Tuesday morning, Susan stayed in bed an extra ten minutes and thought through the situation, trying to create a helpful set of attitudes and feelings. She said to herself, "This will possibly be an unpleasant experience. People will probably be justifiably upset, and they may get angry at me even though this situation was caused by the developer. But this is the reality. I have to accept it, deal with it, and handle it effectively.

"How can I achieve the best results? I'll need to understand the buyers' feelings, listen to their reactions, and not take them personally. If I stay calm and professional, they will calm down too. Then I can explain all the benefits and savings of the presale arrangements and show them why it's still to their advantage to buy.

"Even with the increased monthly payment the owner-occupant is getting an upgraded unit, tax savings, and equity buildup, which outweigh the advantages of renting. If I handle the reactions well, I know many of them will not cancel the contract."

Susan wrote some notes on 3x5 cards, highlighting the key thoughts she wanted to remember and review before each call. In capital letters she wrote, "DON'T TAKE IT PERSON-ALLY," "LISTEN, LISTEN, LISTEN" and "IT'S STILL A GOOD DEAL FOR THEM." Then she took a few extra minutes to rehearse mentally what she was going to do. Creating a mental picture of the first call, she saw herself thinking, feeling and responding in the manner she knew would be helpful. She visualized the buyer calming down, listening, and deciding to go ahead with the purchase.

Susan also prepared herself mentally for difficulties by using a technique called "stress inoculation." She imagined the buyer getting angry at her and saw herself growing defensive in a way that would hurt her chances of success. Then she pictured herself noticing her upset and regaining her composure by thinking productive thoughts and refocusing on her objectives.

She rehearsed mentally in this way until she started to feel confident.

While driving to work, Susan listened to some motivational tapes and then to music that gave her a sense of well-being and optimism. At her desk she reviewed the cards she had written at home, as well as three cards that she read every day before she started work. They contained lists: "The benefits, rewards, and enjoyable aspects of my sales career"; "My strengths as a saleswoman"; and "My personal and professional goals."

Susan completed the first phone call with fairly good results. The buyer was more upset than she expected, but she handled it well. She had an opportunity to explain why she felt it would be in his best interests to go ahead with the purchase. The buyer concluded by saying that he wanted to discuss it with his wife, but that they probably would buy even at the new interest rate. Susan ended by apologizing for the circumstances, reinforcing his tentative decision and setting up an appointment to confirm it later in the week.

After she hung up Susan said to herself, "Hey, I did really well. Now before I make the next call, let me go over what I liked about this one so I don't forget to do it again. Also, I want to review it and see if I can improve."

During the next week Susan contacted all her buyers. Only two canceled, and she resold those units the following week. The vice-president of sales noted her successful response to this difficult situation and four months later she was promoted to sales manager at a new project.

Make It Personal

You may have liked some of the strategies Susan used, and I'm also sure you would have done some things differently. In this situation they worked for her, and I think you will applaud her effort to direct her thoughts and manage her feelings in a difficult situation. She is definitely a learner.

In the chapters that follow I will explain techniques that are used successfully every day in some form by thousands of salespeople. Still, I strongly encourage you to follow Frank Sinatra's motto, "I did it *my* way."

These techniques and self-talk examples are guidelines. Try them out and apply them, but don't hesitate to alter them to fit your own special style and situation.

PART I

Self-Talk, Emotions, and Sales Performance

CHAPTER ONE

The Most Influential Person in Your Life

There is a person with whom you spend

more time than any other, a person who

has more influence over your growth than

anyone else. This ever-present companion

is your own self. This self guides you,

belittles you or supports you.

You engage this person in an ever-constant

dialogue—a dialogue through which you

set goals for yourself, make decisions, feel

pleased, dejected or despondent. In short,

your behavior, your feelings, your sense of

self-esteem and even your level of stress are

influenced by your inner speech.

—Pamela Butler

Talking To Yourself

THE MOST INFLUENTIAL person in your life is you. You talk to yourself throughout your waking hours, and this self-talk has an immediate and profound effect on your feelings, actions, and overall performance.

What is the influence of self-talk on your sales career? Pamela Butler points out that we can create both positive and negative results with our self-communications.

As salespeople we are likely to talk to ourselves before, during, and after sales contacts, sometimes helping ourselves and sometimes hurting our chances for success.

Here are two examples of self-talk creating problems for a salesperson.

Corporate Insurance Sales

Ted R. has put together a corporate insurance package and pension plan for the ABC Company. He is presenting the final package to the president, Mr. Brown, who is responding favorably. Just before he signs the contract, however, Mr. Brown says, "Oh, by the way, my lawyer is here on some other business, and before I give the final approval, I'd like to have him take a look at your proposed plan."

As Mr. Brown goes out to get his lawyer, Ted recalls that three months ago, in a similar situation at another company, a lawyer came in and killed the deal. Mr. Brown and his lawyer return, introductions are made, and the lawyer begins to review the proposal and ask the salesman some questions.

Ted says to himself, "I can't believe it. After all this work, I'm right at the one-yard line and this lawyer is going to kill the deal just like the last one did. These guys always look for a way to say no." He starts to get frustrated and acts defensive when the lawyer begins to ask him questions.

Resort Real Estate

In the early summer of 1985, President Reagan's proposals to revise the tax system received continuous coverage in newspapers and magazines. Many articles made financial projections and recommendations that were generally discouraging to real estate investors, particularly those interested in resort real estate.

Jim L., a real estate salesman at a resort near Charleston, South Carolina, was upset by the media coverage. He found himself thinking, "Gloom and doom is an understatement! Why don't those idiots write about something they know about instead of trying to take money out of my pocket? I might as well pack it up for a while. There's no sense in even calling my clients because they will all want to sell what they have. No one is going to buy with this tax bill pending."

During the next two months Jim's sales manager observed that Jim was frequently out of the office, often playing golf. When he was present he complained often and blamed the tax bill for his poor results.

These salesmen reduced their chances of success by talking to themselves in these ways. Ted created tension and defensiveness, and Jim drastically lowered his motivation to sell. They generated emotions that worked against them and blocked their sales effectiveness. This is called "making a problem out of a problem." Later in this book you will learn methods for eliminating these patterns from your sales career.

Sales Mastery Is Based Upon Self-Mastery

In *Sales Cybernetics*, Brian Adams says, "The professional salesman is an individual who has come to terms with his own self; one who has learned to control his emotional responses:

fears, frustrations, anxieties and moods."

Adams is reminding us of something all salespeople know: sales success depends on mental and emotional factors which require specific thinking and self-management skills.

Consistent top performers are good at what they do, know why they are good, and have learned to make their emotions work for them, not against them, in sales situations.

Your Inner Coach

For a moment, think about the best coach, teacher, or counselor you've ever known. Think of someone who knew just what to say to guide, encourage, and motivate you or to help you bounce back from disappointments.

With the help of this book you can develop your own inner "coach," who will take *positive control* of your self-talk and your emotions. This coach will know you—your good habits and your bad ones; your strengths and where you need to improve; the attitudes and emotions that help you perform and those that block you.

This coach will know what to say—to prepare you mentally for your best sales effort; to reduce fear, anger, and discouragement; to deal with pressures; to get you back on track and help you improve. This coach will help you develop –mental toughness––the ability to perform consistently during adverse conditions. Finally, this coach will teach you to enjoy what you do.

Once this inner coach knows how to influence you positively, key words will quickly trigger the attitudes and feelings you need. For example:

relax	firm	commitment
smooth	flexible	control
concentrate	influence	choice
service	mentally tough	friendly
learner	persistence	
problem solver	improvement	

Mental Skills and Peak Performance

Sales and business contain many examples of super successes who use this inner coach and encourage us to develop one; Tom Hopkins, Larry Wilson, Earl Nightingale, Zig Ziglar, Napoleon Hill, W. Clement Stone, and many others.

In the world of sports we often see highly dramatic models of mental toughness, consistency, and the use of inner skills. Fran Tarkenton, who holds NFL records for total passes, completions, and yardage, prepared for each game by visualizing a wide variety of possible game situations and how he would handle them. Pete Rose could write a book (and I hope he will someday) on his mental approach to baseball. He has a lot to tell all of us about handling pressure, not wasting time and energy on events you can't control, and how top performance starts with enjoying what you do.

Muhammed Ali changed boxing and other sports forever by bringing the mental aspect of competition to the forefront so dramatically. By psyching himself up, he mesmerized opponents with his self-confidence.

Billie Jean King is often credited with breaking the ground and creating the conditions for women's tennis to achieve its current status. She not only blazed the path; she stayed on it, playing successfully into her forties. Billie Jean regularly practices meditation, concentration, and relaxation techniques to develop an inner calm on the court. They obviously helped her in "the battle of the sexes" against Bobby Riggs, professional hustler and psych-out artist. After Riggs had unnerved and defeated Margaret Court, Billie Jean took up the challenge, remained unflappable, and beat him on national TV.

Salespeople rarely approach the drama of Frazier and Ali in the fifteenth round or the excitement of Fran Tarkenton scrambling away from a herd of linemen. Yet, the salesperson faces real struggles to yield results for his company, his customers, his family, and himself. Like all true professionals, the salesperson competes with himself in a complex and demanding occupation.

How You Feel Is How You Sell

In *How to Master the Art of Selling*, Tom Hopkins states, "Positive emotions trigger sales; negative emotions destroy sales." Every salesperson knows intuitively that this is true because your emotions not only affect your actions and skills, *they influence the feelings of your prospect or customer.* Sales is an emotional business, but not all our emotions help the sales process.

The commercial jingle claims, "Things go better with Coke." Sales go better with certain emotions, while other emotions make a hard job almost impossible.

THE TEN MOST WANTED AND THE TEN LEAST WANTED EMOTIONS

I've asked thousands of salespeople to list the ten most helpful emotions they feel while selling and the ten most harmful, which they would like most to avoid. Their answers were very consistent.

The Ten Most Wanted Emotions

- Friendliness and liking people

- Enthusiasm about product

- High energy level

- Enjoying what they do

- Confidence, optimism

- Feeling of being in control

- Relaxed alertness and concentration

- Feeling of wanting to help people and provide service

- Inner desire to persist, succeed, and excel

- Openness and nondefensive attitude toward feedback, criticism, and new informaton.

The Ten Least Wanted Emotions

- Unfriendliness and irritability

- Frustration and anger

- "Down" feeling or depression

- Worry

- Tension and anxiety

- Feeling pressured

- Feeling of not being in control

- Harried, distracted feeling

- Cockiness, over-confidence

- Pessimism about self or product

Effects of Positive Emotions

The salespeople believe that the positive emotions have these effects:

—Creating in the salesperson a readiness to use his skills and knowledge.

—Creating in the customer feelings of relaxation, trust, confidence in the salesperson, and enthusiasm for the product.

—Enabling a salesperson to persist positively and to close a sale.

—Helping a salesperson to develop mental toughness to deal with the challenges and stresses of selling.

—Fostering an openness to feedback, self-critique, and new learning, which lead to continuing improvement.

Effects of Negative Emotions

They see the negative emotions as creating the following problems:

—Making it difficult to establish rapport, reduce interpersonal tension, and build a comfortable, professional relationship with a prospect.

—Detracting from concentration and attention to detail, such as picking up the cues and clues that help them understand the prospect and his needs.

—Blocking the creativity and flexibility that a salesperson needs to respond to the unique, changing pattern of each sales interaction.

—Reducing the positive persistence necessary to work through sales resistance, objections, and indecision.

—Triggering negative feelings in prospects that knock out chances for a sale.

If you were going to bet on a salesperson, which list would you like him or her to be selling from? Obviously people have made sales while in negative moods. On the other hand, having the appropriate emotions doesn't guarantee sales. But selling is a game of percentages, and creating an ideal inner climate stacks the odds in our favor.

We are going to focus on how to spend less time selling with negative feelings and more time selling with appropriate, helpful emotions. By taking more control over your inner life, you will learn how to feel the way you want to feel more often. In any situation, these are the two keys to control:

—You can choose what you say to yourself.

—You can choose what you focus on.

Now we will see how these choices make an immediate, dramatic impact on sales performance.

CHAPTER TWO

Sales Achievement Cycles: Which Ones Do You Create?

Freedom is the awareness of alternatives

and of the ability to choose.

—Alan Wheeler, *How People Change*

WHAT WE BELIEVE and say to ourselves quickly and strongly influences our feelings and actions. In a typical sales contact there is a continuous cycle of interaction involving the self-talk, emotions, and behavior of the salesperson and the customer.

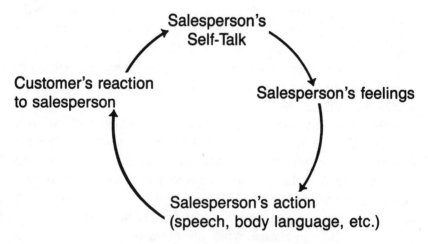

Figure 1. The cycle of interaction in sales

This interplay can spiral towards positive results—trust, respect, confidence and credibility or negative outcomes—poor rapport, tension, and blocked use of skills and knowledge.

Although it's important to acknowledge that we can't control all the elements of this sales cycle, we can learn to master ourselves. We can take the time to take control of our self-talk and create cycles of sales success.

The Underachievement Cycle

Recall Ted, the insurance salesman whose dilemma was described in Chapter 1. You read about his negative reaction, which started to create problems between him and the company lawyer. Figure 2 on page 12 shows how this interaction becomes a vicious cycle underachievement.

We see that Ted evaluates the situation on the basis of a previous experience. He mentally pictures losing the sale again and tells himself it's going to happen. This image triggers frustration.

CASE #1: CORPORATE INSURANCE SALES-MAN AND THE COMPANY LAWYER

Our emotions are reflected in our eyes, face, muscles, and body language. In this case, Ted's face and body tighten up and he feels tense. When asked questions, he displays irritation toward the lawyer and a general defensiveness in his answers.

What do lawyers generally do when someone is defensive in answering their questions? Like most lawyers, this one will probably increase his determination to dig deeper into the proposed plan. If this occurs, in light of Ted's emotional state, he is likely to conclude that he was right. The whole cycle will become even more negative than it is already.

This sequence did not have to happen. Ted could, and did, learn to handle these circumstances differently.

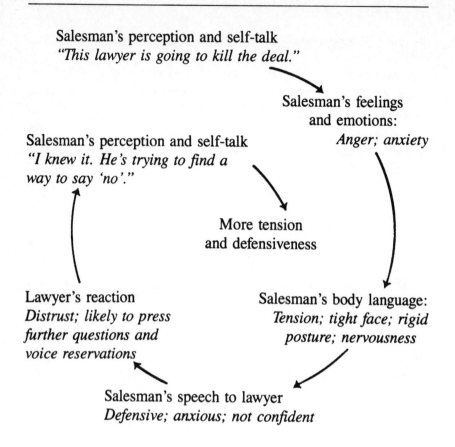

Salesman's perception and self-talk
"This lawyer is going to kill the deal."

Salesman's feelings
and emotions:
Anger; anxiety

Salesman's perception and self-talk
*"I knew it. He's trying to find a
way to say 'no'."*

More tension
and defensiveness

Lawyer's reaction
*Distrust; likely to press
further questions and
voice reservations*

Salesman's body language:
*Tension; tight face; rigid
posture; nervousness*

Salesman's speech to lawyer
Defensive; anxious; not confident

Figure 2. The underachievement cycle.

The Achievement Cycle

The same power of cycles to produce positive momentum
can be seen in Figure 3, as we look at the sequence of reactions
that might occur if the salesman used more helpful self-talk.

If the salesman noticed his tension level rising, for example,
he could say to himself, "Stay calm and professional. This man
is simply doing his job, representing his client, and asking questions. I put a lot of work into this proposal and got the best legal
advice from our home office. My best approach is to be confident and helpful in answering the questions I can answer."

The positive cycle shown in Figure 3 is likely to follow the
salesman's self-talk, although I stop short of saying that the pos-

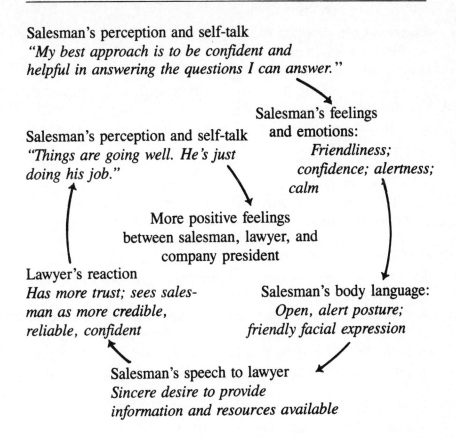

Salesman's perception and self-talk
*"My best approach is to be confident and
helpful in answering the questions I can answer."*

Salesman's feelings
and emotions:
*Friendliness;
confidence; alertness;
calm*

Salesman's perception and self-talk
*"Things are going well. He's just
doing his job."*

More positive feelings
between salesman, lawyer, and
company president

Lawyer's reaction
*Has more trust; sees sales-
man as more credible,
reliable, confident*

Salesman's body language:
*Open, alert posture;
friendly facial expression*

Salesman's speech to lawyer
*Sincere desire to provide
information and resources available*

Figure 3. The achievement cycle.

itive self-talk "made" the sale. The self-talk doesn't guarantee the sale, but by setting into motion the feelings, body language, and behavior of openness, friendliness, and confidence, the salesman greatly increased his chances of receiving a favorable response from the lawyer.

In this situation, which is taken from real life, the salesman noticed his negative self-talk and changed it. In addition to making the sale, his plan impressed the lawyer so that he gave the salesman several referrals of other companies he represented. You, too, can learn to take charge of your self-talk and turn around the demanding situations you face every day.

Exercise: Sales Scenarios

Here are eleven other incidents that salespeople have shared in my seminars. The situations cover all stages of the sales process in a wide variety of locations and industries. In each case I've described events up to the point that the salesperson uses self-talk. At that point I've left a space for you to write down your own reaction.

This is a very important activity. We can change mental habits and patterns only if we are aware of them. Take this opportunity to learn about sales self-talk and increase your awareness of your own probable reactions to these situations.

Put yourself into the salesperson's shoes. How would you react and respond? Spontaneously, without censoring your thoughts, write down what you would say to yourself if you were that salesperson in that situation.

This is a tested method, which thousands of salespeople in our seminars have used to begin learning about their own mental environments. If you do this in an honest, direct manner you will receive clues about how you really go through the sales process.

Be especially alert for *patterns* of self-talk that you can identify. At this stage, don't concern yourself with changing your self-talk; just observe it.

After you've written down your reaction, go on to read the two examples of other salespeople responding to the same situation. A major purpose of this activity is to highlight the salesperson's alternatives in each situation. Study this self-talk along with your own and try to visualize what kind of cycle each self-talk might create.

As a reminder, this symbol will appear after each case study:

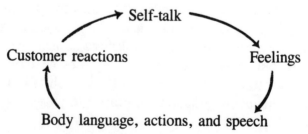

CASE #2: THE STOCKBROKER AND
THE ENTREPRENEUR

A little over a year ago, Jane S. began her career as a stockbroker for a major firm that offers a wide variety of products and financial services. She has been moderately successful to this point, establishing clients among her friends, family contacts, and some company-generated leads. Her current clients have yearly incomes that range from $25,000 to $75,000.

Last week, a friend gave Jane a referral; Mr. Clark, who has started and sold several businesses and currently owns a very successful manufacturing company with 250 employees. Jane's friend has given Mr. Clark her name and told him that Jane would be contacting him.

Your self-talk:

Self-Talk: Jane #1

"This is probably going to be a waste of time. He earns ten times as much as I do, and for all I know, he started his first business before I was born. How will he ever respect anything I say? If he's nice, he'll just patronize me; if not, this will really be embarrassing. He'll never trust me with his money."

Self-Talk: Jane #2

"My friend said that Mr. Clark is totally devoted to his business which is growing rapidly. This is just the kind of person that I can be the greatest help to. He probably doesn't have the time or knowledge to maximize the management of his personal investments. I work for an excellent firm that offers the range of products he needs. I'm constantly studying and I'm aware of the market, tax changes, and new financial products. I can work harder than anybody for Mr. Clark."

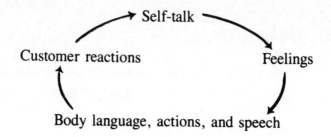

Self-talk

Customer reactions

Feelings

Body language, actions, and speech

CASE #3: PROSPECTING BY TELEPHONE

The XYZ Company has developed and initiated a direct-mail campaign to generate leads. The sales staff is a vital part of the program, and they are expected to make 150 to 200 follow-up calls in the week after the letters are delivered.

Past results have indicted that the evening is the best time to call to make appointments. One of the XYZ salespeople is about to sit down and begin calling.

Your self-talk:

Self-Talk: Salesperson A

"I hate this. People don't want to be disturbed at night and they talk to you like you're a creep. I'm going to miss the Cubs game—for what? Nothing ever comes from these calls anyway."

Self-Talk: Salesperson B

"Well, this probably isn't the most fun part of the business, but I've often heard that in sales, if you do the things no one else likes to do, you'll really go far. The company spent a lot of money on this mailout and they're providing me with an opportunity to generate customers.

"I know some people won't be interested and some are a little resistant to phone calls like this, but the product and the offer will appeal to a lot of people. I'll just be relaxed, friendly, and courteous to reduce their tension and then set up appointments.

"I'm sure the sales manager will notice my effort and my results."

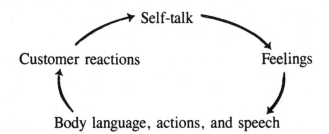

CASE #4: THE BAD START

Joe C. is a salesman for a pharmaceuticals firm and has a three-county territory near his home. Last night, Joe went to a party, drank a little more than usual, and got to sleep a little later than usual. This morning he wakes up late and somewhat groggy.

As he rushes to get ready, he cuts himself shaving. He decides to skip breakfast, and just takes a mug of coffee with him to drink as he drives to his first appointment. As he backs out of his driveway, Joe enters the traffic faster than he should and has to hit his brakes. The coffee spills over his shoes, his socks, and the bottom of his pants.

Your self-talk:

Self-Talk: Joe #1

"What a disaster! I'm going to look like a real slob at Dr. Johnson's office. I can see already this is going to be one of those days where nothing goes right."

Self-Talk: Joe #2

"I'm off to a heck of a start today. I'd better stop and get myself together or I might blow the whole day. I'll just have to see Dr. Johnson a little late, with a nicked face and coffee stains. I'm not the first guy this has happened to and I probably can make a joke out of it. We have a pretty good relationship. After I see him, I'd better get a real breakfast. I can still make this a productive day."

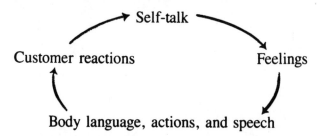

CASE #5: THE PESSIMISTIC SALESWOMAN

Gerri and Susan are residential real estate saleswomen with a small firm in the suburbs of Washington, D.C. One morning, when Susan is at her desk, Gerri comes in looking depressed. Gerri complains, "Did you read that article about the real estate market? It's a shambles. Real interest rates are the highest in history and nobody is buying anything because they're waiting to see the new changes in the tax law. Who knows when that will be? They keep getting paychecks on Capitol Hill, but in the meantime, you and I will starve to death!! Little firms like ours can't make it in this market."

Your self-talk:

Self-Talk: Susan #1

"Wow, she's right. I read that article, and it really is 'gloom and doom' for our industry. This article will put the final nail in the coffin because everyone will know how bad it is. Why did I have to pick this time to try to sell real estate? I'll have to eat crow and ask for my word-processing job back."

Self-Talk: Susan #2

"I've read the article, and I'm adjusting my sales strategy based on current realities. This situation could be a great opportunity. It's the very reason I need to work smarter and harder. There have to be sellers out there who will read this article and want to move their property now, before the law changes. Also, there are always sharp buyers who take advantage of a situation like this and are willing to take some risks if they can buy discounted property.

"I need to use my time and energy to plan and act, and I'm not going to buy into Gerri's discouragement."

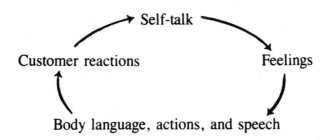

CASE #6: PROBLEMS DURING THE SALES PRESENTATION

A computer salesman has been working to make a large sale to the managing information systems (MIS) department of a division of a Fortune 500 company. He has designed an elaborate presentation to deliver to the key decision makers in the MIS department.

While giving the first half of the presentation, the salesman decides that it is not going well at all. His audience is not responding positively, their body language is discouraging, and their questions seem somewhat hostile.

Your self-talk:

Self-Talk: Salesman A

"I'm bombing! I'm blowing the whole deal. These cold, dead fish are really getting me uptight, just staring at me. Wait till my manager hears about this. He'll never let me present a big deal again by myself. God, I wish this was over!"

Self-Talk: Salesman B

"Things are not going well. I thought they would receive this much more positively. I've got to find out what they are reacting to—the proposal itself or how I'm delivering it? I'd better stop at a logical point and make a sincere effort to get their honest feedback so that this can focus better on their needs. If I can work in a break, maybe I can get one-on-one with some of them and find out exactly what's going on. Then I can make some improvements.

"OK. Take a deep breath, dig deeper, and concentrate."

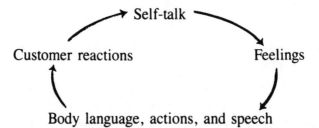

CASE #7: AFTER MAKING THE SALE

Roberta L. sells advertising for a radio station in a small northeastern city. For the past three weeks, she has been working toward selling a large amount of advertising time to a local chain of restaurants. On Friday afternoon, the vice-president of

the chain calls and tells her that her proposal has been approved
and they want to buy the time she suggested. After working out
some details and thanking him, Roberta hangs up.
Your self-talk:

Self-Talk: Roberta #1

"I got it! This calls for a celebration. I'm going to call Joe
and take him out to eat in our favorite restaurant."

Self-Talk: Roberta #2

"I got it! This calls for a celebration tonight. While this sale
is fresh in my mind, I'd better take a few minutes to go over
and write down what I did right. What steps did I take?
What were the factors under my control that contributed to
this sale? I don't want to have to reinvent the wheel every
time, so what do I want to make sure I do again in this type
of situation?"

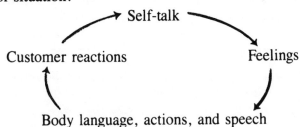

CASE #8: AFTER LOSING THE SALE

A large real estate development corporation has built a new
resort in a Sun Belt state. The resort is located at a considerable
distance from current travel patterns, and the corporation has
decided to use a variety of incentive marketing programs to
bring prospective purchasers to the resort. Currently they are
selling lots, patio homes on a golf course, and time-sharing
villas.

The marketing program is effective, and many visitors come to obtain the incentives (such as trips and cameras) and to see the resort. The on-site sales force consists of nine men and women, including John H., who has toured fifteen couples in the last two weeks without making a sale.

Today he has taken another couple on a sales tour, and again he has failed to make a sale. After the couple has left, John is walking back to his office.

Your self-talk:

Self-Talk: John #1

"These people don't want to buy. All they do is come up here for some freebies and waste my time. What a pain! And how am I supposed to sell anything with the way they are developing this place? There's construction crap all over. It looks like a war zone. They've got all these number crunchers running things and nobody knows what they're doing."

Self-Talk: John #2

"This is bad. I'm zero for two weeks. I can't pass this off as bad luck or bad prospects, because some of the other people are making sales. If I start putting these prospects down or taking my frustrations out on them, I'll really dig a hole for myself. I'm in a slump. I've been in slumps before and I'll get out of this one, but I've got to get some feedback about what I'm doing.

"All these 'nos' I'm getting show me I'm off track, but I need to identify the specifics I need to change. I'm going to ask Ann about her approach because she seems to be doing pretty well. I'm also going to go through my entire presentation and strategy with Dan and get his feedback."

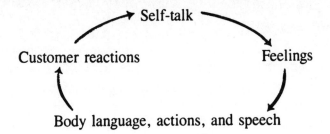

Self-talk

Customer reactions   Feelings

Body language, actions, and speech

CASE #9: THE BOSSY SECRETARY

Sam H. sells dental supplies in a fairly large territory. His travel schedule includes quarterly visits to the dental offices in a certain area.

Doctors Jones and White have a substantial practice, and their head secretary, Mrs. Kyle, is also the office manager. Mrs. Kyle tends to be very solicitous to patients, protective of the dentists' time, and not very friendly to salespeople. In talking to salespeople, she usually takes on a somewhat authoritarian tone and conveys that she is doing them a favor by letting them talk to the dentists.

Sam arrives at the Jones-White office for his quarterly sales call and announces to Mrs. Kyle that he'd like to meet with either of the dentists to discuss their product needs. Mrs. Kyle asks him rather coldly to have a seat in the waiting area. She says she will tell the dentists that Sam is there, and she adds, "However, patient care obviously comes first."

As Sam sits down in the waiting room . . .

Your self-talk:

Self-Talk: Sam #1

"Who does she think she is? The Queen of England sitting on a throne? She treats me like dirt every time I come here. She always gets me so upset that she throws me off for the whole day. Her little power trips really push my buttons."

Self-Talk: Sam #2

"No one can dictate how I will feel today except me. No one can push my buttons but me. Mrs. Kyle is not very friendly, and she's definitely showing me she has some control around here. I doubt she has anything personally against me; she's probably trying to do what she thinks is in the best interests of the dentists and their patients. Dr. Jones always speaks very highly of how she runs the office, so I guess she's here to stay.

"My best strategy is to try to understand things from her point of view. This will help me calm down. Maybe I can ask her for her suggestions on how I can complete these quarterly visits in a way that minimizes the interference with patient service, but also allows me to provide the products Dr. Jones and Dr. White need."

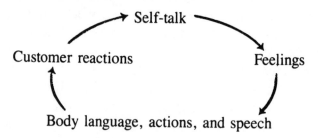

CASE #10: THE "TYPICAL" OWNERS

A wine salesman is going to visit Mr. and Mrs. Ortega, who have recently purchased a small grocery store within his territory. He is meeting them for the first time, and he wants to make sure they keep his displays and try a case of his new wine and juice product.

Your self-talk:

Self-Talk: Salesman A

"Well, this is another one of those typical Mom-and-Pop operations. I've seen a hundred of them. This won't take long. I'll show them what we've been doing in their store and the other stores like theirs, and then set up the new product display."

Self-Talk: Salesman B

"People who own small grocery stores have some similarities, but each set of owners is unique. Before I push my line on them, I'd better find out as much as I can about them. Are they new to this business? Do they know the neighborhood well? Are they aware of their competition? Do they have any ideas already about wine sales and displays? This is a good opportunity to show them how I can help them and give value-added service."

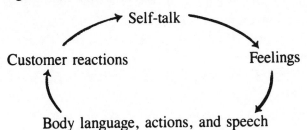

Self-talk

Customer reactions

Feelings

Body language, actions, and speech

CASE #11: THE CANCELED ORDER

The Excello Manufacturing Company is part of a network of corporations owned by 3X, a $12-billion multinational firm. Ron H., a salesman for a training company, has put together a $100,000 participative-management and quality-circles training package for Excello, which has been approved by the vice-president of human resources department.

Today Ron is meeting with the vice-president to discuss the procedure for introducing the training. When Ron arrives at the meeting, the vice-president informs him that regrettably, he has to cancel the proposed training.

Financial restrictions imposed by the president have affected the training budget, and the training requisition was vetoed this morning. A total budget freeze has been established.

Normally, the vice-president's approval guarantees a contract, but in this case the decision is out of his hands.
Your self-talk

Self-Talk: Ron #1

"He can't do this. This double-talking guy caved in and blew the deal. How can they run a business like this? They can't treat me this way after all the work I did."

Self-Talk: Ron #2

"What a lousy break! That really hurts! I've always heard this can happen in our business, and it just happened to me. I've done a lot of good work here and I don't want to waste it. I need to focus on what I can salvage in this situation.

"First, I have to establish whether this cancellation is only due to this budget crunch or whether there's some other objection or consideration. If it turns out that this vice-president really likes this training package, that can be very useful.

"My objectives now are to keep him open to this package and to leave an opening to presenting other products in the future. Also, I can get his recommendation on the training proposal and present it to the referrals he can give me in other divisions of 3X."

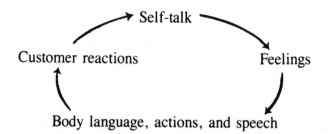

CASE #12: THE DISTRACTED CAR SALESMAN

Ralph M. sells new cars and trucks for a large, busy dealership near Atlanta. He works the showroom, and in rotation with other salesmen, he greets and tours prospects who walk through the door.

This morning Ralph has a couple of things on his mind. When he came to work, there was a message on his desk that one of his customers had decided to buy a foreign car from another dealership instead of the car Ralph had showed him last week. In addition to this, a local businessman has been considering buying a company car, a personal truck for his minifarm, and an economy car for his son. The businessman's accountant is reviewing the price, down payment, and monthly payment figures that Ralph provided, and Ralph expects to hear today whether or not the businessman will go ahead with the purchase.

Ralph is sitting by his phone when the sales manager signals that the people coming through the door now are his responsibility.

As he gets ready to meet them he is thinking . . .
Your self-talk:

Self-Talk: Ralph #1
"When will the government stand up for us and stop letting these Japanese imports beat our brains in? I had that sale in the bag. Well, maybe I can make up for that and more with a triple sale. I can't wait to hear from that accountant. It's nerve-wracking waiting on such a big sale."

Self-Talk: Ralph #2
"The only people who can help me reach my sales goals *right now* are the people who just walked through the door.

I can't make any sales *yesterday*, and I can't do anything about the triple sale or the Japanese import problem at this moment. I need to give these folks my full attention and concentration. Right now, they are the most important people in my sales world."

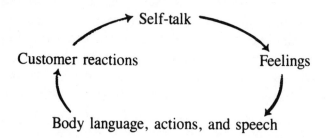

Self-talk

Customer reactions

Feelings

Body language, actions, and speech

Exercise: Your Sales Experiences

To move from someone else's experience to your own, review your experiences in sales. Think of two situations, one positive and one negative, where your self-talk and emotions affected the results. Write out the circumstances; your self-talk, feelings, and actions and the outcome for each situation.

Situation 1: positive results
Circumstances:

Your self-talk:

Results:

Situation 2: negative results
Circumstances:

Your self-talk:

Results:

Negative Self-Talk Patterns

You have now seen that some self-communications are more helpful than others. I've listed the most common types of ineffective self-talk and nonproductive thinking and provided examples from the cases you have just read.

Ineffective Self-Talk	Consequences
I can't	Discouragement, pessimism,
I can never . . .	giving up, self-downing,
I'll never be able to . . .	frustration
He'll never . . .	
They always . . .	
Exaggerations and	More intense upset, no focus
magnifications	on improvement
Name-calling	More inflamed feelings
She made me [upset]	Anger, absence of "win-win"
He's making me . . .	behavior, potential for conflict
	Loss of control
It will be awful, terrible,	Worry
horrible . . .	
I can't stand . . .	Frustration, anger

Figure 4. Ineffective self-talk.

Nonproductive Thinking	Consequences
Jumping to hasty conclusions and making quick inferences	Tendency to go beyond facts and trigger stronger reactions; tendency to see fewer alternatives
0 to 100% either/or thinking	Blocks out possibilities for improvement and learning; demotivates
Believing you should be able to control others	Frustration and anger
Overpositive, unrealistic expectations	Failure to anticipate appropriate problems and do proper planning; discouragement when expected results don't occur
Overgeneralization; making negative evaluations based on one or two events	Over negative perspective

Figure 5. Nonproductive thinking patterns.

SALES EXAMPLES

Case #1

Jumping to negative conclusions: "This lawyer is going to kill the deal."

Catastrophizing: "After all this work, I'm right at the one-yard line."

"Always": "these guys *always* look for a way to say no."

Case #2

0-100% thinking: "going to be a waste of time."

Catastrophizing: "This is going to be embarrassing."

"Never": "He'll *never* trust me."

Case #3

Overgeneralizing: "People don't want to be disturbed . . . they talk to you like you're a creep."

0-100% thinking: "*Nothing* ever comes from these calls anyway."

Case #4

Exaggerating, magnifying: "What a disaster!"

Name calling: "—look like a real slob."

Jumping to conclusions: "—going to be one of those days where nothing goes right."

Case #5

Jumping to quick, negative conclusion: "—will put the final nail in the coffin."

Exaggeration: "—because *everyone* will know."

Catastrophizing: "I'm going to have to eat crow."

Case #6

Exaggeration, catastrophizing, quick conclusions: "I'm bombing. I'm blowing the whole deal."

Name calling: "—cold, dead fish."

They make me upset: "They're making me feel . . . getting me uptight."

"Never": "He'll *never* let me."

Case #8

0-100%: "These people don't want to buy. All they do . . ."

Name calling: "—construction crap, war zone, number crunchers."

Exaggeration: "*Nobody* knows what they're doing."

Case #9

Name calling: "Queen of England sitting on a throne."

Exaggeration, "always": "She treats me *like dirt every* time."

She makes me upset: "She *always* gets me upset . . . she throws me off for the *whole* day."

Case #11

Control, they shouldn't do: "He can't do this . . . they can't treat me this way."

Name calling: "—this double-talking guy."

Self-Talk Patterns

Initially it is difficult for most people to notice their self-talk. That's why I've invited you to write down your self-talk and then examine it. This is the best way and, in many instances, an essential way to become aware of your self-talk patterns.

In later chapters you will be learning a great deal more about both positive and negative thoughts, but now it's important to extract some knowledge about yourself.

Exercise: Self-Awareness

Review the self-talk responses you wrote after each case above, as well as the positive and negative example you described from your own sales experience. *Underline* the self-talk that you think would be useful and circle the self-talk that would create attitudes or feelings that might hurt your performance.

If you notice any patterns, list them below.

Useful self-talk patterns

Nonproductive self-talk patterns

CHAPTER THREE

Thinking About What You Think About

As a man believeth in his heart, so he is.
—Proverbs 23:7

Winners control the flow of their self-talk.
—Dennis Waitley, *Seeds of Greatness*

Take charge of your thoughts. You can do what you will with them.
—Plato

THESE TWELVE CASES and your own sales examples show that there are alternative ways to think in every situation, and the choices really matter.

Many of you are probably saying, "It doesn't seem like a matter of choice. **That's just the way I react.**"

Is that true? Are our reactions automatic and out of our control, or can we really choose and decide how we will respond?

You probably have figured out my answer to these questions. If I believed we had little or no control over our thoughts, this would be a very short book!

This idea becomes clearer when we realize that many of our thought patterns and emotional reactions are HABITS.

Learning About Habits

Let's do some simple experiments. First fold your arms on your chest in the way that feels most comfortable. Now fold your arms again but reverse the top arm and bottom arm.

Now take a pen and paper and sign your name the way you normally do. Then sign it again, but **skip every other letter**. This way requires only half the physical work, but it takes twice or three times as long.

These quick experiments can teach us the following about habits:

- Habits are comfortable.
- Habits are automatic. We don't have to think about them.
- Habits are not easy to change.
- We're not always aware of what habits we have.

How do these ideas apply to our thoughts?

BELIEFS and ATTITUDES = MENTAL HABITS

We Are Creatures of Habit

Like all habits, mental habits are learned and repeated, and often become automatic. When we first learn to drive we are strongly aware of each movement. After we've mastered the skills, however, we drive by habit, acting automatically and not even aware of the steps involved unless we choose to notice them.

The same is true for our beliefs and attitudes. They are well formed and often repeated, and we tend to not even be aware of them. We don't think about what we think about . . . . think about that! Marshall McLuhan once said, "I don't know who discovered water but I'm convinced it wasn't fish."

Mental Habits

This lack of awareness about our surroundings is also true of our beliefs. We tend to respond automatically and not to notice how our thoughts contribute to our feelings. It's natural not to think of yourself as choosing your thoughts because the habits and patterns are rooted so strongly. The thoughts seem just to happen, with little influence from us.

In some ways we are like the worker who sat down at noon and opened his lunch pail to find a peanut butter and jelly sandwich. He exploded, "I can't stand it. Every single day the same crummy lunch; peanut butter and jelly, peanut butter and jelly!" His buddy said, "Why don't you tell your wife to make something else?" He replied, "Oh, I make my own lunch."

Still, we all know that habits can be changed. Each one of us has altered old habits and acquired new ones, whether in sales, bowling, or thinking. We have done it (1) when we became aware of the habit; (2) when we became convinced it was blocking us from reaching our goals; (3) when we worked at substituting a new, more useful habit.

Some of our beliefs are very helpful and reinforcing. Others can be self-defeating and harmful. Millions of women in our society, for example, suffer from anorexia nervosa, bulimia, and other forms of eating disorders. Millions more are convinced that they're too heavy, and don't like their appearance. Studies show repeatedly that these women have internalized the belief, "The only attractive woman is a thin woman. I must be thin. I'm not thin enough."

Obviously, not all our mental habits and emotional patterns help us in life or in sales, but I hope this discussion about beliefs and habits has raised some questions in your mind. "What are my mental habits and patterns? How can I become aware of them? How can I change them and learn new, helpful attitudes and inner skills?"

The key to answering all these questions is SELF-TALK.

SELF-TALK IS THE KEY

to awareness

to motivation to change

to self-mastery

Listening to Self-Talk

Fortunately, there is a very simple way of learning about our thoughts, beliefs, and attitudes. It's based on the fact that we all talk to ourselves a great deal of the time.

Have you ever listened to your "mind chatter"? Do you tune into that channel? If you do, one thing you notice immediately is how rapidly your mind works. Research shows that while normal conversation with another person is conducted at about 125 to 150 words per minute, self-talk speeds on at rates of 400 to 600 words per minute; 400 to 600 words per minute of instructions, criticism, comment, and dialogue with yourself. What is the effect of all this self-talk?

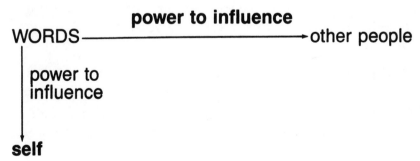

Figure 6. The power of words.

Dr. Maxie Maultsby points out (Figure 6) that we are implicitly aware that words have power because we often make an effort to choose our words when speaking to others. We know that words influence feelings, so we choose them to facilitate our interactions. Salespeople say:

agreement, not *contract*
investment, not *price*
valued at, not *costs*
involved, not *sold*
presentation, not *pitch*

because words create mental images, arouse emotions, and affect decisions.

If we agree that words have power, what about the words we use when we talk to ourselves; do those words have a powerful effect on us?

GIGO

A useful starting point in our understanding is the analogy of the brain as a computer. Our ten billion brain cells have often been described as a supercomputer, but like all computers, they follow the law of GIGO: garbage in, garbage out.

The computer won't say, "I know you didn't mean to program me this way. I'll change it around for you." It will simply process the program you put in.

Our brains work in the same way. In twenty years of working with individuals in all types of settings I've found that people—myself included—often say irrational, illogical, exaggerated, and unhelpful things to themselves and never question any of it.

Take the Time to Take Control

What must you do to increase your positive programming? Take the time to gain control over the flow of your self-talk.
1. Listen to your self-talk. All your beliefs and patterns can be found in your self-talk.
2. Discover how your self-talk affects your feelings and performance. Once you really see the negative effect, you will be strongly motivated to change.

3. Get off "automatic pilot." If you don't, your habits will repeat themselves and grow stronger, and you'll feel that you have no control. You have a choice in every situation, and you can learn to exercise that choice.

4. Acquire positive internal skills and high-achievement attitudes. Make them your new mental habits.

In the chapters that follow, I will present positive, useful self-talk. I will also give you guidelines and techniques to make sure the self-talk that works for you becomes a new mental habit.

As you go through the activities, skills training, and examples, I suggest you make notes about these questions:

What are my mental habits and emotional patterns?

How do they help or hurt me when I sell?

What self-talk and mental skills would I like to have in sales situations?

Choosing our Focus

We can not only choose what we say to ourselves in a situation; we can also select what we *focus* on. Focus influences strongly how we think, feel, and eventually act.

In *Zen and the Art of Motorcycle Maintenance*, Robert Pirsig tells us about focus in this way: "We take a handful of sand from the endless landscape of awareness around us and call that handful of sand the world."

We select our focus but we are almost never aware of the choice we make or of the alternative choices that are possible. Our focus shapes our awareness and consciousness. Because no one else can choose the contents of our mind, we must be the ones to make these choices. Yet in daily life we tend not to see how important "focus" is in determining how we feel and react. We tend not to notice that we are focusing on some aspects of our environment and not on others.

Our habitual patterns seem to be the "natural," the "normal," and sometimes the only way to look at things.

If we return to our case studies and look more closely at the self-talk responses, we can see that in many instances the first response differed from the second not only in self-talk but in focus. Note the dramatic, significant differences.

Case #1: Corporate Insurance Sales

Ted #1 (focus)

Ted #2 (focus)

Past experiences with lawyer; the future: "This lawyer is going to kill the deal."

Maintaining positive feelings; the present task of answering questions

Case #2: The Stockbroker and the Entrepreneur

Jane # 1 (focus)

Jane #2 (focus)

Reasons why phoning Mr. Clark is fruitless

Reasons why Mr. Clark needs her products and services

Case #3: Prospecting by Telephone

Salesperson A (focus)

Salesperson A (focus)

The negative aspects of this type of prospecting

The benefits and rewards of completing the task; the specifics of effective execution of the task

Case #4: The Bad Start

Joe #1 (focus)

Joe #2 (focus)

What has gone wrong

The humorous side of his disasters; good relationship with Dr. Johnson

Case #5: The Pessimistic Saleswoman

Susan #1 (focus)

Susan #2 (focus)

Everything that is wrong; the future failures: "I'll have to eat crow and ask for my word processing job back."

Current realities; solutions, opportunities, and effective planning

Case #6: Problems During the Sales Presentation

Salesman A (focus)   *Salesman B (focus)*

Picturing failure and negative criticism

Discovering areas that need to be improved; steps to correct the current situation and learn from it; managing emotions

Case #7: After Making the Sale

Roberta #1 (focus)   *Roberta #2 (focus)*

Celebrating

What she did effectively that she wants to repeat

Case #8: After Losing the Sale

John #1 (focus)   *John #2 (focus)*

What's wrong with the prospects and the developers; blaming and excuses

Current realities; past successes; obtaining specific feedback that will lead to improvement

Case #9: The Bossy Secretary

Sam #1 (focus)   *Sam #2 (focus)*

What's bad about the secretary; how she upsets him

Understanding the secretary's behavior; planning effective strategy for dealing with her and achieving goals

Case #10: The "Typical" Owners

Salesman A (focus)   *Salesman B (focus)*

What he usually does

Understanding the unique aspects of this customer in this situation; providing value-added service

Case #11: The Canceled Order

Ron #1 (focus)   *Ron #2 (focus)*

What is being done to him   What can be salvaged from
                                   this situation; obtaining a
                                   recommendation; referrals,
                                   an opening to present future
                                   products

Case #12: The Distracted Car Salesman

Ralph #1 (focus)   *Ralph #2 (focus)*

Japanese import problems;   The customers who just
pending triple sale   walked through the door

As these examples demonstrate, our focus contributes directly to our results. Our goal is to learn how to take charge of our focus and how to build the mental habits that enable us to focus in useful directions throughout the sales process.

Focus is a key to success in every performance arena. One crucial difference between mediocre poker players and the top professionals is that when the pros are dealt a hand, they scan it quickly and then direct their attention to the other players. They concentrate on details and nuances that give them clues about the unique quality of this hand. Mediocre players pay too much attention to themselves and their hands and miss these vital cues that would improve their strategy.

In this way sales performance is similar to results at the poker table. The consistently successful sales professionals have finely tuned guidance systems. They focus most of their energy on understanding the uniqueness of each customer and using this information to reach their sales objectives.

Realistic Thinking, Focused on Improvement, Versus "Positive" Thinking

The approach you are about to learn differs in important ways from current views of positive thinking. This chart shows the differences:

SELF-TALK

Negative thinking
(Gloom and doom)
_____
Positive thinking
(Rosy, sometimes
unrealistic, may not
plan for real problems)

Realistic appraisal,
(plans for maximizing
results in any situation,
focuses on possibilities
and improvement)

Figure 7. Realistic thinking.

These approaches are illustrated in three possible speeches a manager could deliver to his sales force upon learning about a significant price advantage achieved by a competitor.

Negative Thinking

"It's a disaster. They are the low-cost producers and I don't know how we can sell against them. This is going to be a bad year for all of us."

Positive Thinking

"We are going to have a great year! I know we will hit our sales goals. You people are the best and I know you can make those sales even with these new prices."

Realistic Thinking, Focused on Improvement

"Our competitor's recent drop in prices gives them a definite advantage in this marketplace. We have our work cut out to achieve our goals, so let's focus on our strengths and advantages. Our research and engineering staffs are going full out to reduce production costs, so I hope this price disadvantage won't continue very long. As I see it, one of our main strengths is customer service and the loyalty we've developed. We need to maintain that and put even more emphasis on it.

"In my opinion, you are a highly skilled sales force. This gives us an edge. Let's build on it."

Positive thinking can be useful in some circumstances, but it can lead to unrealistic optimism. When expected results are not forthcoming the optimism can collapse like a deck of cards. In addition, if we rely too heavily on positive thinking, we may not anticipate some of the significant obstacles in our path.

In *Intrepreneuring*, Gifford Pincast III describes this aspect of successful entrepreneurs:

> Another part of the entrepreneurial strategy for reducing risk is anticipating barriers and remaining open to feedback, both positive and negative. Entrepreneurs are not Pollyannas or exaggerated devotees of positive thinking. While they have great confidence they can overcome them, they are aware of and seek information on the risks and problems. Venture capitalists see this fact as a screening device for selecting who to back. Entrepreneurs who cannot see problems or imagine how anything might go wrong are seen as promoters, not as real entrepreneurs.

The skills and guidelines outlined in later chapters blend realism and optimism. They are oriented toward obtaining the best results in every situation.

We are now ready to learn and apply self-talk principles to each stage of the sales process. They include maximizing our chances of success through proper preparation as well as improving rapidly by using helpful self-talk and focus after each sales contact.

THE PATH TO "THE WINNING EDGE"

Before the Sale
- Professional sales preparation
- Mental rehearsal
- Positive self-motivation

During the Sale
- Positive focus and concentration
- Managing FEAR, ANGER, and DISCOURAGEMENT
- Self-management skills

After the Sale
- The self-talk of learning and improvement
- Your Sales Performance Profile

PART II

Before the Sale

CHAPTER FOUR

Professional Sales Preparation

If you don't know where you are going, any road will take you there.

When we plan, we don't just plan FOR the future, we plan so that we will HAVE a future.

DURING THE UNITED States Olympic qualifying trials, a study was conducted to determine the mental factors that contribute to achievement. Weight lifters were interviewed, and significant differences were found between the qualifiers and the nonqualifiers in the way they prepared mentally for the competition.

Those who succeeded in qualifying devoted considerable preparation time to these four areas of mental and emotional preparation:

1. Increasing self-confidence
2. Sharpening focus and concentration
3. Creating the proper energy level
4. Visualizing the desired performance

Most of us have been told all our lives about the importance of preparation, but how often have we been trained to prepare effectively? Unfortunately, the typical situation is a process of trial and error; a salesperson picks up some helpful techniques, and if he or she is not too busy or too distracted, may use them in preparing for a sales contact.

The Only Time You Have Total Control

In professional tennis or racquetball the server will often determine the outcome of the point. By the same token, baseball is said to be 70 to 80 percent pitching.

The only time that the player has total control is before the serve or the pitch. That is the moment to shape the event and maximize the opportunity for success. The pros take advantage of that special situation.

The same is true in sales. Before the sales contact, the salesperson can "seize the moment." Through proper mental preparation and planning, he or she can create ideal attitudes and emotions for performance. This is the chance to improve the percentages and "put the ball in play" in a way that will optimize the results.

Two Key Elements

The most effective preparation usually includes two elements. The first is taking the time to create the attitudes and feelings that you've learned help you perform at your best. The second is gathering information and planning for this specific situation.

Professional Sales Preparation	=	Creating your top performance attitudes and feelings + Customizing your strategy to the specifics of this sales contact

Successful preparation requires having clear, specific goals; deciding on the attitudes and emotions that will help you achieve those goals; and using self-talk that will create the inner climate you need to perform.

The Preparation Form

The Professional Sales Preparation Form below provides a step-by-step format for developing these techniques. In the example given below, the sales person is Jane S., the stockbroker who is calling on Mr. Clark, as described in Case #2 (page 15). Jane lists her goals for this situation, which include how she wants to feel and act as well as the result she wants to achieve during this phone call. She reminds herself of the attitudes and emotions that will help her perform, and then writes out the self-talk that is likely to make her feel the way she wants to feel.

Before Jane picks up the phone to call Mr. Clark, she uses this self-talk. She repeats it to herself slowly and meaningfully, and within two or three minutes she feels ready and eager to make the call. Later, as she masters this preparation sequence, she can customize her self-talk each time without using the form. Professional sales preparation becomes a positive mental habit that often takes only a few minutes.

PROFESSIONAL SALES PREPARATION

Purpose: To determine the attitudes, feelings, actions, and self-talk that will prepare you best for a specific sales activity.

Directions: Select a specific sales activity and complete the Professional Sales Preparation Form for that situation.

Situation: (Interview, presentation, sales call, handling objections, customer complaints, closing, obtaining referrals)

Calling on Mr. Clark, a successful businessman, for the first time.

Goals: 1. Remain relaxed and confident.
2. Identify Mr. Clark's needs for my products and services.
3. Focus on the benefits that my firm and I can provide.
4. Arrange an appointment to meet with Mr. Clark.

Appropriate emotions and attitudes that will help you reach your goal:
1. Relaxed concentration
2. Confidence in myself and my firm
3. Desire to help Mr. Clark and confidence that I can.
4. Enthusiasm
5. Friendliness

Useful self-talk:
Mr. Clark is totally devoted to his business, which is growing rapidly. This is just the kind of person that I can be of the greatest help to. He probably doesn't have the time or knowledge to maximize the management of his personal investments. I work for an excellent firm that offers the range of products he needs. I'm constantly studying, and I'm aware of the markets, tax changes, and new financial products. I can work harder than anyone else for Mr. Clark.

Other actions: Listen carefully.

Every salesperson's career is unique in many ways. Companies, products, services, commissions, marketing, and prospecting all vary, and each of us has our own style of selling, a blend of our skills and our personality.

I encourage you to discover the self-talk and preparation sequence that works best for you. At the end of this chapter you will have the opportunity to complete your own Professional Sales Preparation Form for a specific contact from your sales world.

First, though, I'm going to show you examples of self-talk that salespeople have found to be consistently helpful and effective. This collection is a starting point; I hope you will go further and design additional self-talk. In this section the self-talk is presented along with the inner goals it is designed to create. In some cases there is additional discussion of key ideas.

As you read each self-talk, repeat it slowly and be aware of how you would feel if you said these words to yourself and believed them. Make a note of any example that you think might be useful for your mental preparation.

SELF-TALK SECTION

Self-Talk #1.
Goals: Sense of being in control; confidence.
"I am taking charge of my inner life by choosing my self-talk. I 'warm-up' mentally by focusing on effective self-talk and I prepare thoroughly for every sales interaction."

Self-Talk #2.
Goal: Friendliness.
"I like to meet people and I focus on their good qualities. My goal is to make each person glad they talked with me."

The more you like your customers, the better your intuition about how to serve their needs.

Gifford Pinchot III,
Intrepreneuring

Self-Talk #3.
Goals: Gratitude; focus on opportunities; enthusiasm.
"I'm thankful to have this opportunity to present myself and my product."

Self-Talk #4.
Goal: Motivation and enthusiasm for prospecting and sales calls.
"Each person I contact has the potential of opening up a world of new customers and referrals."

Self-Talk #5.
Goals: Focus on customer's needs and perspective; adjustment to uniqueness of each situation; calm.

"I can never control other people, but I can influence them. If I want to influence their decisions and actions most effectively, I need to listen to them, understand them and be able to see things from their perspective. I ask myself, 'What is special or unique about this customer or this situation?' and I let this question guide me."

Self-Talk #6.
Goals: Concentration, elimination of distractions; calm; patience.
"The best person to help me reach my sales goals is the customer or prospect I'm going to contact right now. The very best use of my time, energy, and skills is to concentrate them on this interaction and focus on one step at a time."

Self-Talk #7.
Goals: Reducing tension; increasing action and risk-taking; focus on learning and improvement; reducing fear of failure confidence; enthusiasm.
"Every day I can learn important things about myself; my products and services; customers and prospects; market conditions and competition; sales process and skills. The cumulative results of gaining useful information from my experiences every day will propel me toward my goals; therefore, I'm not afraid to try and I'm eager to learn and improve."

This self-talk is part of a key attitude associated with sustained high levels of achievement; Stewart Emery calls it "the attitude of a learner." This focus on improvement and extracting learning from experience not only leads to rapid development of sales expertise; it also provides an antidote to the stresses and rejections inherent in selling. We will explore this point in later chapters, but for now we will emphasize the importance of willingness to act, risk, and put forth full effort without being discouraged.

This attitude is expressed in an anecdote shared by Arthur Gordon, at the time an aspiring writer. He asked Thomas J. Watson, the president of IBM, for advice.

"It's not exactly my line," Watson said, "but would you like me to give you a formula for writing success? It's quite simple, really. Double your rate of failure.

"You're making a common mistake. You're thinking of failure as the enemy of success. But it isn't at all. Failure is a teacher—a harsh one perhaps, but the best. You say you have a desk full of rejected manuscripts? That's great! Every one of those manuscripts was rejected for a reason. Have you pulled them to pieces looking for that reason?

"You can be discouraged by failure—or you can learn from it. So go ahead and make mistakes. Make all you can. Because remember that's where you'll find success. On the far side of failure."

A wise and tolerant man had given me an idea. A simple idea, but a powerful one; if you can learn to learn from failure, you'll go pretty much where you want to go.

—Arthur Gordon,
On the Far Side of Failure

Another key quality of learners is the constant search for information that will give them the winning edge, the ability to perform at a higher level in each situation.

Pete Rose is one of the most prominent examples of the "learner" approach in baseball. One anecdote, which shows the learner in preparation, involves the catcher for the Atlanta Braves.

In the 1984 season Pete Rose was 43 years old, had played in the major leagues for over twenty years, and had already produced over 4,000 hits. Before a game with Atlanta, while Pete was chatting nonchalantly with the Braves' catcher, he asked casually if Rick Mahler, Atlanta's scheduled pitcher for the next day's game, had been throwing his knuckleball much lately.

If Pete Rose, a professional and a recognized star with twenty years' experience, is still searching for useful information before he performs, what are the implications for you as a salesperson?

What can we learn about our prospects, customers, competitors, or market conditions that will be helpful in preparing for sales interactions? Brian Adams advises all salespeople to recognize themselves as market researchers. This image of yourself will keep you alert for key information.

The knowledge of the marketplace possessed by salespeople is a valuable resource. In November 1985, Ray Easterlin, president of Heritage Properties, decided to ask for advice from the Dunes Marketing Group salespeople who were selling his condominium project in Palmetto Dunes Resort on Hilton Head Island.

Jim Moore and Gary Greenip from Dunes Marketing led a brainstorming session, trying to find out what changes the salespeople thought Easterlin needed to make to get sales moving again. They generated a list of suggestions which, if followed, would interest buyers.

Easterlin listened and made the changes, and in a hectic four-day burst during the Thanksgiving weekend, 21 condominiums were sold for a total of $3.8 million.

This is just one example of the salesperson's power as a market researcher.

Self-Talk #8.
Goals: Confidence; self-esteem
"My strengths as a salesperson are . . ."
a) presentation skills
b) listening skills
c) ability to read people
d) ability to think and react quickly
e) ability to organize workload
f) writing skills
g) previous success patterns
h) skills of persuasion
i) sincerity and trustworthiness
j) solution orientation
k) capacity for hard work
l) good appearance
m) ability to stay positive

n) energy and enthusiasm
o) mental toughness
p) relaxed attitude
q) professional demeanor
r) optimal aggressiveness
s) desire to close
t) action orientation
u) attitude of a learner
v) other strengths

Each of us possesses a variety of personal strengths and resources. It is very important for salespersons to remind themselves regularly of their strengths. This procedure serves as an antidote to the rejections and discouragements in sales, and helps a salesperson to separate his self-esteem and self-worth from his recent results.

Review the list above and add any others that you consider important. Then make a check mark next to each strength that you feel you possess. A "strength" is an area in which you are reasonably proficient and which contributes to your success. Therefore don't eliminate an area for consideration just because:
a) you don't use the strength all the time;
b) you feel you can and should improve in this area;
c) you can think of people who are stronger than you in this area;
d) you overuse this strength.

None of these facts should prevent you from acknowledging that you have this strength, even though you still want to improve.

After you've decided what your strengths are, discuss them with your sales manager or another salesperson. You may wish to make adjustments to your list and add new strengths that you discover through selling. List your strengths on a card for easy reviewing.

This "strength recognition" is very helpful when you've reacted to recent results by being excessively down on yourself. You can also apply it in a situation that is more difficult or challenging than usual.

Self-Talk #9.
Goals: Enthusiasm; enjoying what you do
"I enjoy what I do because of . . ."

a) work environment
b) sense of being a competent professional
c) opportunity to meet new people
d) earning power
e) contributing to my company's financial well being
f) opportunity to help people
g) the challenge of selling
h) a chance to test how good I really am
i) the opportunity to develop myself through training, coaching, and self-education
j) recognition from peers and managers
k) camaraderie on the sales team
l) freedom to achieve through my efforts
m) other reasons

In every endeavor, the individuals who love what they do and continue to enjoy it are invariably among the highest achievers. Our prospects and customers pick up our enthusiasm and enjoyment, and they like to do business with us.

Yet, in the heat of the battle, even those who enjoy a job may lose sight of what they like about it and begin to focus on the negatives.

Review the list above and check each item that you consider a real plus in your selling career. Add any specific benefits of your current job and any other important long-range goals that sales will help you achieve.

Write this complete list on a card and look at it every day. This list will strengthen your desire to sell and your love of selling. You will develop further your "will to win."

Air Force officers who conduct survival training for pilots consistently report that the individuals who make it home are those who have a burning reason to survive. The reasons vary: self-preservation, ego drive, competition, family and loved ones, responsibility. Salespeople can build "the will to win" by focusing on the rewards and goals of sales success.

Self-Talk #10.

Goals: Attitude of service; focus on customers' needs, problems, and goals.

"I want to help people meet their needs and solve their problems. I'm always alert to their stated needs and goals, and I look for opportunities to use my knowledge, skills, and contacts to help them. I welcome the chance to demonstrate that I'm willing to go the extra mile in their interests."

The ability to understand the customer's needs and wants can be summed up in a simple phrase: "Always be learning."

—Karl Albrecht and Ron Zemke,
Service America

This "attitude of service," which is tied closely to the "attitude of a learner," is an essential ingredient in long-term, consistent achievement in sales because it leads to strong customer relationships and many referrals. In *The One-Minute Salesperson,* Spencer Johnson and Larry Wilson describe this attitude as "the wonderful paradox": "I have more fun and enjoy more financial success when I stop trying to get what I want and start helping people get what they want."

Norman Vincent Peale relates that one of his early mentors was a merchant, Emil Geiger, who taught him something about selling that influenced his ministry from its inception. Geiger, for whom Peale worked as a youth, told him, "Create the image of yourself as someone who cares about the customer, not about the customer's money, and you will always do well."

Customer service is the sales and marketing strategy of the future as well. "The trend toward consumerism, the changing competitive climate and the recent recession all have forced companies to reexamine their relationships with customers. As a result, customer service has become a strategic tool. It used to be regarded as an expense. Now it is seen as a positive force for increasing sales—and for reducing the cost of sales" (Warren Blanding, editor, *Customer Service Newsletter*).

This attitude and approach deserve a high priority, and self-talk #10 is a useful reminder before each sales interaction.

Self-Talk #11.
Goals: Confidence in the benefits of your product and services; enthusiasm; focus on how the benefits fit this particular customer.
"My products and services will benefit *this* customer because . . ."

Develop a list of all the different benefits and advantages that you, your products, and your services deliver to your various customers. Review it regularly.

When you're meeting with a prospect or customer for whom you already have information about needs, problems, and goals, review your list of benefits and emphasize mentally those that are probably most important for *this* customer.

For any product or service, your most important sales goal is to sell yourself. Salespeople need to be sold and resold to maximize their enthusiasm and effectiveness.

Dave "Moose" Bosson, one of the best salesmen and sales managers I've had the good fortune to know, always spells "enthusiasm" this way:

EnthusIASM

Dave is aware of the need to maintain a fresh, positive perception of his products, and capitalizing IASM is a reminder that enthusiasm develops because I AM SOLD MYSELF. I have seen him launch several highly successful sales campaigns by "selling" one or two key members of his sales team.

Self-Talk #12.
Goal: Reduction of pressure, tension, and nervousness.
"This is *one* sales contact. It's important to me, but it's also important to put it in perspective. No one sales interaction determines my self-worth or competence as a salesperson."

Nervousness and tension reduce effectiveness for a variety of reasons. In addition to blocking us from using our skills, they often cause prospects to lose confidence and trust in our competence.

The major goal is to consider the current situation important but not earth-shaking. There are many ways to remind yourself to put your current performance in proper perspective; self-talk #12 is one of them. It's useful for each salesperson to find the self-talk that helps strike this balance between motivation and counterproductive pressure, self-talk #12 contains some useful guidelines.

One of the most memorable self-talks I've found is that used by Tug McGraw when he was a relief pitcher for the New York Mets. Upon entering a crucial game in the late innings with men on base, McGraw would breathe deeply and say to himself before he pitched, "A hundred years from now, no one will give a damn whether this guy hits a home run or strikes out." In this important situation, McGraw didn't have to motivate himself to perform. He needed to relax himself and reduce the "catastrophe" mentality.

Self Talk #13.
Goal: Confidence, energy.
"I'm ready. I've done this successfully before."

Personalize Your Preparation

Take the time to discover and develop the mental preparation pattern that will work for you every day.

A resort real estate salesman in Sarasota, Florida, takes thirty seconds to look at the beautiful Gulf of Mexico before he goes downstairs to meet prospects. For him, it's a quick review, on a deep level, of the benefits of owning property at his resort. He reminds himself of how much pleasure and relaxation people enjoy by owning property and vacationing there.

A manufacturer's representative for a pipe fittings company in Michigan pauses before each sales call to focus on a sense of gratitude and responsibility. He recognizes the opportunity and is grateful for a chance to present himself and his product. Then he thinks about foreign competition and its impact on his company. He reports that it increases his determination and persistence when he focuses on this sense of responsibility to his company and its employees.

A female energy sales consultant, who works for a New York State gas and electric utility company, calls mostly on men who are not accustomed to women in this industry. She has designed specific self-talk that prepares her for each call and reduces tension and frustration.

When I am selling, training, or writing, I prepare by pausing thirty seconds to be grateful for this opportunity, to present myself, my products, and my ideas. I remind myself that it is a privilege to have the chance to make a difference in people's lives. This pause helps me feel good about myself and my career, and friendly toward the people I am about to meet.

Finding your best style is an ongoing process. Be alert for phrases or sayings that could become a useful part of your mental environment. Begin by completing "Important Self-Talk for My Sales Preparation," which appears below. Review the self-talk section in this chapter and write down whatever you think may be useful in the "Helpful Self-Talk" column. For each piece of self-talk, indicate the desire, feeling, or attitude you want to create.

REVIEW: IMPORTANT SELF-TALK FOR MY SALES PREPARATION

Desired Attitude/Feeling   *Helpful Self-Talk*

On the next page you will find a Professional Sales Preparation Form. Choose an actual sales situation and complete the categories: goals, appropriate emotions and attitudes, useful self-talk. Three extra copies are included to help you prepare for key sales calls and presentations in the future.

Exercise: Professional Sales Preparation

Purpose: To determine the attitudes, feelings, and self-talk that will prepare you best for a specific sales activity.

Directions: Select a specific sales situation and complete the Professional Sales Preparation Form.

Situation: (interview, presentation, sales call, handling objections, customer complaints, closing, obtaining referrals)

Goals:

Appropriate emotions and attitudes that will help you reach your goals:

Useful self-talk:

Other actions:

Exercise: Professional Sales Preparation

Purpose: To determine the attitudes, feelings, and self-talk that will prepare you best for a specific sales activity.

Directions: Select a specific sales situation and complete the Professional Sales Preparation Form.

Situation: (interview, presentation, sales call, handling objections, customer complaints, closing, obtaining referrals)

Goals:

Appropriate emotions and attitudes that will help you reach your goals:

Useful self-talk:

Other actions:

Exercise: Professional Sales Preparation

Purpose: To determine the attitudes, feelings, and self-talk that will prepare you best for a specific sales activity.

Directions: Select a specific sales situation and complete the Professional Sales Preparation Form.

Situation: (interview, presentation, sales call, handling objections, customer complaints, closing, obtaining referrals)

Goals:

Appropriate emotions and attitudes that will help you reach your goals:

Useful self-talk:

Other actions:

Exercise: Professional Sales Preparation

Purpose: To determine the attitudes, feelings, and self-talk that will prepare you best for a specific sales activity.
Directions: Select a specific sales situation and complete the Professional Sales Preparation Form.

Situation: (interview, presentation, sales call, handling objections, customer complaints, closing, obtaining referrals)

Goals:

Appropriate emotions and attitudes that will help you reach your goals:

Useful self-talk:

Other actions:

When you've determined the self-talk you want, the next goal is to make it part of your inner life. How do you establish new mental habits and thinking patterns? How do you acquire new attitudes and ways of approaching the sales process?

You've taken the first steps. Now it's time to learn how to make the progress permanent with positive programming that will become part of you.

CHAPTER FIVE

Relaxation, Visualization, and Mental Rehearsal Techniques

The most successful sales tool I have ever

found is imagining the desired outcome.

—Joe McKinney, CEO, Tyler Corporation

HABITS ARE FORMED through repetition. Although we're aware of the countless repetitions of physical habits, like the way we shave, drive, or sign our name, we seldom notice our repeated mental patterns. Yet each of us has patterns of self-talk and beliefs that we've reinforced tens of thousands of times.

When we attempt to change our mental habits, we encounter resistance. Dr. Maxie Maultsby compares this to a jockey's experience trying to ride a horse that is accustomed to another rider. The jockey may have clear intentions about how he wants the horse to behave, but the horse has been trained to react in a different fashion. Like the horse, we have our patterns. Our brain cells, neural connections, limbic system, glands, and muscles are "wired" in established ways. Yet just as the horse can be retrained with patience and persistence, we can be reprogrammed; our neuromuscular habits can be changed. Human beings can be "de-patterned" and can learn to think differently.

One key to making new self-talk a permanent part of our inner vocabulary is *repetition*. It's unrealistic to expect the horse to change after one command, and just as unlikely that we will acquire new mental habits instantly.

Repetition and reinforcement can be achieved in a variety of ways. The most effective ways for salespeople are cards, audiotapes, posters, signs, symbols, and visualization.

Cards

After establishing helpful self-talk, many salespeople like to write it on 3x5 cards that they can review often.*

Here are some guidelines for using the cards:

1. Work on a small number of cards (five to ten) during a concentrated three-week period.
2. Two or three times a day, read each card slowly and allow yourself to experience the feelings that follow the words.
3. Continue this process for three weeks and practice the new self talk in real situations as soon as possible.
4. After three weeks introduce new cards and repeat the process.
5. Continue to review the previous cards twice a week.

Audiotapes

Many salespeople use motivational and educational audiocassettes in their cars, offices, and homes. This is an excellent method for acquiring new self-talk. Individuals can benefit from packaged self-talk tapes as well as creating tapes in their own voice, customized to specific goals.

These are some guidelines for using tapes:

1. Concentrate on a limited amount of new self-talk for a three-week period.

2. Listen to the tapes two to four times a day.

3. The best listening times are upon waking, when going to bed, or during periods of quiet and relaxation.

4. Use the tapes to prepare yourself as you are driving to a sales call or before telephoning prospects and customers.

---

*All the self-talk examples mentioned in this book are available on cards and cassettes in the "Self-Talk: The Winning Edge in Selling" card system and cassette series. A description of the training package is provided on page 160.

Posters, Signs, and Symbols

We are all triggered and "programmed" to some degree by our environment. The input of newspapers, TV, movies, and coworkers, as well as other elements in our environment, invariably influences our thoughts, feelings, and actions. One way to take charge of our inner life is to be more aware and then more selective about the external messages we want to receive.

It's very helpful to restructure your environment so that it supports the productive attitudes and thoughts you want to have. Be alert for posters, pictures, signs, or objects that are meaningful reminders for you, and use them in your office, home, or car.

Most individuals find that the more personal these reminders are, the more effectively they help you maintain your desired attitudes. When I went through rigorous training in Japan twenty years ago, for example, my teacher often stressed the word *neridashi* (endurance) while he coached me. This word came to have special meaning for me; now, whenever I need to remind myself to make a sustained effort on a long project (like writing this book), I hang a "–NERIDASHI–" sign on my office bulletin board. It has a powerful, positive effect on my determination.

Search your thoughts and your environment for these reminders and make them a more consistent part of your everyday life.

Visualization

If we made an informal survey of the self-help, business, and sports sections in bookstores, we might conclude that visualization and mental imagery are new techniques for personal and professional development.

Actually we are already familiar with the process of visualizing because each of us, to a certain degree, creates pictures or mental images in our minds. Some of us create more vivid images, but all of us can and do use our imaginations.

When we worry, for example, we usually have a mental picture of a terrible result. We think about this event and imagine that it might happen; our nervous system responds with tension and fear. When we relate this picture to our performance, such as a sales call or a presentation, we are actually holding what Dr. Sandy Smith refers to as a "dread rehearsal." Mentally we "rehearse" all the awful things that are going to happen, and we start to convince ourselves and our nervous system they *will* happen.

The secret to visualization is that our brains react to vivid images with almost the same intensity as they would to a real-life situation. In addition, our mental images provide a "road map," a guidance system for our mind-body system. Maxwell Maltz made this the basis for his pioneering work *Psychocybernetics,* encouraging us to tap this ability in order to direct ourselves towards our goals.

The results of both positive and negative mental imagery have been well documented in sports, from basketball foul shooting to downhill skiing to high jumping. A recent Olympic medalist in target shooting used visualization techniques exclusively to prepare because his arm was injured. His results actually surpassed his previous performances, although he had fired very few shots before the competition.

An experiment in mental imagery and golf putting demonstrated that our visualizations can quickly help us or hurt us. Controlled groups of competing golfers were instructed to call up different mental pictures before each putt. One group imagined the ball going right into the cup; the other group pictured the ball going straight to the cup and then off to the side. The first group consistently outperformed the "negative" visualizers.

How can we use visualization to help us as salespeople? First, it's important to be aware of negative images and try to change or eliminate them. My friend "Dot" Grover Bolton told me of an experience that illustrates this point.

As an undergraduate at Syracuse University, Dot was a national baton-twirling champion, and she received the opportunity to perform in the Orange Bowl. As she walked into the empty stadium the day before the game, she thought, "What if I drop the baton in front of 80,000 people?" The image devastated her, and she realized quickly where that road would take her. Immediately she changed her mental picture and thought about her successful past experiences. She told herself that she would be just as good the next day, and she was.

Visualization also gives us a vehicle for unlimited practice. We can mentally rehearse our desired actions over and over, in great detail. The ideal performance becomes clear and crystallized, and this makes it much easier for us to perform just as well in real situations. We have a detailed mental blueprint for success.

You can reinforce new, productive patterns of self-talk, feelings, and sales effectiveness. To help you create these new patterns, you will learn visualization techniques to deal with all phases of the sales process: preparation, managing problems and upsets, handling rejection, and much more.

Relaxation Exercises

The essential foundation for effective mental rehearsal is relaxation, and the ability to relax deeply is a valuable skill for salespeople in its own right. It can help you reduce the cumulative stresses of selling. Some people use it to provide an oasis of calm in an otherwise turbulent day.

Relaxing before visualization is vital, because the mind is more open to new learning when it is calm and relaxed. New ideas, thought patterns, and internal responses are accepted more easily and then integrated on a deeper level. The new "programming" more readily becomes a part of us, not merely words that we say to ourselves on a superficial level.

Relaxation aids the flow of images and makes it easier to channel thoughts in desired directions. There are countless techniques and exercises for relaxation, in addition to the individual ways each person has developed. We will focus on four techniques which millions of people use regularly. Each of these techniques has been used successfully and effectively by salespeople, and we are providing them to support visualization techniques as well as your overall sales career. Most people find them simple and pleasant.

As with any skill, practice is required to achieve mastery. I suggest that you try each of these techniques and stay with one or two that are most comfortable and useful for you. Sometimes an individual doesn't like the experience of "letting go" that's associated with some of these methods. If this turns out to be true for you, simply relax yourself in a way that's comfortable for you when you use relaxation in conjunction with the mental rehearsal techniques.

1. The Peaceful Place. A very common technique, which most people are able to adopt, makes use of our previous experiences with relaxation, peace, or tranquility. You simply imagine an ideal place of relaxation. The place or scene will vary; it may be some place you've been, possibly a childhood spot, or even a place you've seen in pictures or movies. Usually it is a natural setting—the seashore, mountains, meadows, or a wooded trail—but it can also be a certain room.

Settle into a comfortable position in a chair, or recline and allow yourself to relax as much as you can. Then visualize your peaceful scene, as vividly and in as much detail as possible. Imagine yourself in the scene, and try to be aware of all your senses and how it feels to be in this place.

Simply allow yourself to relax and enjoy the quiet and tranquility and pleasure of this scene. Five to ten minutes is a good length of time to begin with.

2. Maltz's Relaxation Technique. Maxwell Maltz recommends a relaxation technique in his classic book, *Psychocybernetics*. The first part of the exercise is similar to "the peaceful place." Then, after you have relaxed with the peaceful scene, you will use your imagination to achieve deeper relaxation.

To begin, imagine that your body is made of lead. Focus on your arms, legs, torso, head, and so on, and imagine that each part is so heavy that you couldn't lift it even if you wanted to. Each part of you is so heavy that the dead weight is sinking deeper into the chair or bed. Continue in this way until your whole body feels very heavy and sinks into what you are resting on.

After a few moments, begin to imagine that your body is becoming very light. Visualize little helium balloons attached to your hands, arms, feet, ankles, legs, head, and torso. Your body is so light that you begin to float gently.

Continue until your body feels as if it is floating effortlessly, with no tension or stress, completely relaxed. Ten minutes is a good initial time period for this technique.

3. The Jacobsen Relaxation Method. This technique, which involves alternately tensing and relaxing muscles, has been used widely for fifty years. It combines awareness of where the body is tense with an understanding of the feelings of tension and relaxation. Each part of the body and each muscle group is tensed and relaxed twice, and relaxation spreads gradually to the entire body. An important benefit of this system is that after you master the technique you can often trigger relaxation by tensing and relaxing just one part of your body, such as your right hand or foot. In this way you can relax inconspicuously in sales situations.

To begin, you need a quiet place with a chair or a bed. Remove your shoes, and loosen any binding or tight-fitting garments, and sit back or lie down.

Starting with one hand, make a tight, tense fist for five to seven seconds and then relax it completely. While you are tensing, be aware of how it feels. Then, when you relax, give yourself the command, "Relax," and feel the warmth and pleasure of relaxation. After ten seconds of relaxation, repeat the tensing-relaxing sequence.

Repeat this two-step process twice with your forearm, bicep, other arm, feet, calves, thighs, stomach muscles, back and shoulder muscles, neck, chin, and face.

Occasionally, if you are fairly tense when you start, you may have to tense-relax a certain part of your body more than twice.

Allow relaxation to spread throughout your body, and continue to heighten your awareness of the different feelings associated with tension and relaxation. It is important to cue your relaxation to the command "Relax" because this cue will become a useful self-management device when you want to relax in sales interactions. The Jacobsen technique takes fifteen to twenty minutes.

4. The Frozen Rope Breathing Technique. The "frozen

rope" is one of hundreds of breathing and concentration techniques which have been used for thousands of years to quiet the mind and achieve tranquility. Other techniques are described effectively in other books, including *The Relaxation Response* by Robert Benson, M.D., and *TM: Discovering Inner Energy and Overcoming Stress* by Harold Bloomfield, M.D.

We prefer the frozen rope because it promotes *the ability to concentrate* as well as relax. People have long used breathing as a way to achieve inner control because it is both a voluntary and an involuntary process. If we choose, we can direct the rhythm of our breathing and influence some of our inner processes, including our level of relaxation and calm.

To begin the frozen rope, sit comfortably and loosen any belts or clothing that would restrict your breathing.

Your goal is to make your exhalations slow and even. Start by closing your eyes, breathing deeply through your nose, and then exhaling slowly and smoothly through your mouth. As you exhale, imagine that your breath is extending like a frozen rope of air. Concentrate on the slow, even flow of air and the picture of the frozen rope.

At the end of the exhalation, wait a couple of seconds before you inhale. Initially this will seem hard, so don't force it; but later, as your breathing slows down, you will look forward to these very peaceful seconds, breathing neither in nor out, but simply sitting quietly and concentrating on the frozen rope of air. When you inhale, allow your body to breathe as quickly and deeply as necessary to fill your lungs. Then begin the slow, even exhalation again.

Five to ten minutes of this breathing and concentration will usually produce good results. As with the Jacobsen technique, an added bonus of the frozen rope exercise is that after you've done it regularly for a while, you can often trigger relaxation with only one to three breaths.

Exercises: Visualization
1. Recreating a previous successful sales call
Goals: to increase confidence; to focus on and reinforce what you did right so that you can repeat it.

In a quiet setting, close your eyes and relax. Mentally picture a sales situation where you performed very competently. Bring back as many details of the sale as you can, including your self-talk, attitude, feelings, actions, and how the customer responded. Let yourself relive the experience. Go through the process at least twice, until you are clear about what you did that was effective and you begin to feel confident.

2. Preparing for a successful sales call

Goals: to build a mental road map of positive results; to instill new self-talk and inner patterns; to practice the way you want to sell.

Select a sales contact for which you are currently preparing. If you completed the Professional Sales Preparation Form in the last chapter, use that situation. Review the details about your goals, your self-talk, and how you want to feel.

Begin by relaxing; quiet your mind by eliminating distracting thoughts. Rid yourself of negative, nonproductive images. Now picture yourself preparing by using appropriate self-talk. Then begin to see yourself feeling just the way you want to feel.

Let the good feelings sink in. Then focus on your actions. Imagine yourself performing with a smooth, relaxed alertness. Then see the prospect or the customer responding with trust and confidence. Picture the sales outcome that you want.

Repeat this visualization of success until the details become clear and vivid.

Visualization is a powerful device that requires practice. Don't give up or be discouraged if you find it difficult initially. This mental skill is a key ingredient in the self-mastery that salespeople need for peak performance. Once you can do it easily and effectively, it will become part of your routine in mental preparation.

If you are trying to create new patterns of self-talk and emotion while you sell, do visualization exercises at least twice a day for three weeks.

CHAPTER SIX

Conquering Procrastination through Positive Self-Motivation

No matter who you are or what your age

may be, if you want to achieve permanent,

sustaining success, the motivation that will

drive you toward that goal must come from

within. It must be personal, deep-rooted

and a part of your innermost thoughts. All

other motivation, the excitement of a

crowd, the stimulation of a pep-talk, the

exhilaration of a passing circumstance is

external and temporary. It will not last.
—Paul J. Meyer, President of Success Motivation Institute

Hope is the passion for the possible.
—William Sloane Coffin

AT THE CLOSE of my Self-Talk sales seminars I always ask the participants what subjects they found useful and what they are going to apply immediately. The most common answer is always, "Techniques to stop procrastinating."

Procrastination is a universal human problem. Salespeople are certainly not immune to it, even though their income and advancement depend on action, not avoidance.

Avoidance is the key element. When we avoid tasks and activities that we know are in our best interests and would help us reach our stated goals, we are procrastinating. In this chapter you will have an opportunity to identify the key areas you avoid; learn why you don't complete certain tasks in a timely manner; and then acquire the self-talk and skills for positive self-motivation.

Procrastination can become something you *used to do*, and you can achieve the satisfying and energizing feeling of moving directly toward your goals.

Dr. Albert Ellis describes three types of procrastination that affect results in our family and work environments:

Personal and professional development
Maintenance
Responsibility to others

Let's explore how each of these types affects a sales a career.

Professional Development

Most of us have some medium- to long-range objectives which would further our careers as well as give us personal satisfaction. Some examples for salespeople include:

- Licenses (real estate, securities, insurance)
- Certification
- Participation in industry groups and boards
- Increasing product knowledge through self-study or courses
- Sales training or sales management training
- Learning about a new product or service area
- Developing a new business wardrobe

- Creating new stationery, cards, advertising, business promotion
- Expanding into new territory or acquiring new types of customers
- Broadening business or technical background

These are just a few of the important, rewarding objectives that many salespeople do not attain because they put off the tasks necessary to reach them.

Maintenance

Many aspects of selling require regular maintenance to insure consistent results. These include:

- Grooming
- Wardrobe
- Health and energy
- Car
- Financial management
- Paperwork
- Prospecting for new customers
- Regular followups to customers
- Newsletters, contacts, etc.
- Planning and scheduling
- Reports
- Reading to keep up with changes in product and market

Neglecting proper maintenance can rob us from reaching our full sales potential.

Responsibility to Others

In many of the examples above, procrastination hurts nobody but us, but in some instances our lack of action is irresponsible to others.

Sales examples might include:

- Not making decisions or taking actions, thereby causing a delay for someone else
- Not completing a proposal or report
- Not doing research or finding information that someone is counting on
- Not responding promptly to letters or phone calls

- Not following through and doing what you've said you were going to do.

The negative effects of procrastination are obvious from the examples above. In addition, people report that the habits of procrastination have negative psychological consequences.

Psychological Effects of Procrastination

Most of us, who are results-oriented and aware of what actions would be productive for us, are not totally at ease when we are avoiding a task. Psychologists have shown that the unfinished task or activity tends to hold some of our attention (the Zegarnik effect). When this is a task that we really feel we "should" be performing, the net results of avoiding it are periodic feelings of distraction, anxiety, and guilt. If we are putting off several things, we may feel harried as they keep popping up in our mind.

In addition, repeated procrastination can easily affect our self-image and our confidence. When we put off moving toward our goals in professional development for long periods of time, we may suffer the feeling of not reaching our true potential or developing our talents. By failing to meet deadlines we can lose the sense of being in charge and moving forward.

Avoidance can also bring feelings of guilt. Even when procrastinators finally act, they often become upset with themselves and say, "Why couldn't I have done that when I was supposed to?" "Look at all the hassle I put myself through by putting it off," or "I put this off so long that I had to rush to get it done and it's really not as good as I could have done."

Now is the time to explore procrastination as an issue in your sales career. (If you don't feel like doing this now, and are telling yourself you'll do it later, you can add this activity to the list of things you put off!)

Exercise: Procrastination in Sales

Review the three types of procrastination, the sales examples for each type and the psychological effects of procrastination. Then complete the form below to identify how procrastination is affecting your overall sales performance.

Exercise: Procrastination in Sales—Personal Inventory

Professional Development
What am I procrastinating about?

How is it affecting my results?

What are the psychological effects?

Maintenance
What am I procrastinating about?

How is it affecting my results?

What are the psychological effects?

Responsibility to Others
Is there anything I am avoiding doing that is irresponsible to others?

How is it affecting my results and my relationship with others?

What are the psychological effects?

Another way of viewing procrastination is to picture it as a "state of demotivation" for a particular task. When we are demotivated we don't want to perform, and when we procrastinate we find something else more desirable to do with our time. What are the reasons we put it off? We'll look at three general categories:

Task characteristics:
    boring
    unpleasant
    arduous
Task consequences:
    fear of
        change
        the unknown
        failure
        rejection
Task controls:
    planning
    scheduling
    reminders

Task Characteristics

Sometimes we are demotivated by the **characteristics** of the task. We might consider it **boring, tedious, repetitious, difficult, or unpleasant**. If we view the task as **beneath** us or we are resentful that we "have to" do it, our motivation is also likely to fade away. This anger is often a powerful hidden force behind procrastination.

Task Consequences

Another key determinant of our motivation is how we view the **consequences** of the task. Fear is a powerful demotivator, and it can block us from action even though we are unaware of it.

When we fear the outcome of a particular task or activity in sales, we usually experience one or more of these fears:
- fear of change
- fear of the unknown
- fear of failure
- fear of rejection

In particular, the following situations can increase fear and thus reduce the motivation for a task:
- a large project
- not being clear on what you are supposed to do

- not knowing how to start
- never having done it before
- having done it and experienced rejection or failure
- hearing about others doing it with negative consequences

Task Controls

A third contributor to the lack of timely action is improper controls for planning, scheduling, and reminding. Improper controls include not allowing enough time, not setting aside periods to do the work, or not developing systems to remind you to act.

Before you can conquer procrastination, it helps to understand the specific reasons why you don't complete an activity. Complete the "Understanding Procrastination" chart by listing the important actions you delay or avoid.

CHART: UNDERSTANDING PROCRASTINATION

Tasks or activities that I put off	*Probable reasons why I procrastinate*

SELF-TALK AND MOTIVATION

Because motivation is what causes a person to act, all motivation is really self-motivation. Each of us decides to act or not on the basis of how we evaluate the consequences. Often our level of motivation is influenced directly by our focus and our self-talk. In fact, demotivation has a specific self-talk language.

Demotivating Self-Talk:

It's boring.
It's too hard.
I hate doing it.
I can't do it.
I'll never be able to do it.
I shouldn't have to do it.
I deserve better than this.
It's too much.
I'll never be able to finish it.
I'll get to it someday.
It's not that important.
They're making me do it.
I have to do it.
They don't treat me fairly, so why should I do this for them?
I don't have to write it down. I'll remember to do it.
I deserve to relax and have some fun, and I'll get to it later.
I've heard it's really a drag and it doesn't pay off anyway.

Although these statements are varied, they have some common threads. Primarily we see a **focus on negatives**; boredom, dislike, pressure, resentment, no confidence of success, no expectation of payoff. As we talk to ourselves in this way, as we focus on everything we don't like about doing it, what are we doing to our level of motivation?

Our power to motivate ourselves works two ways. We can develop and strengthen our ability to motivate ourselves positively, and in doing so we take tremendous strides in overcoming our inclination to put things off.

The Self-Talk of Positive Motivation

"I remember standing next to him one day when it was around 100 degrees out and somebody was groaning about having to play a doubleheader in the heat," Frey once recalled.

"Musial turned to me and said, 'Little guy, do you know what this doubleheader means today? It means Stanley has a chance to get ten hits today. Ten hits!' Here the other guy is griping and Musial's thinking ten hits.

"I remember before one game, the Cardinals are taking batting practice and everybody's yelling, 'Stan, Stan, Stan.' He tips his cap and bows to them and says softly to me, 'Little guy, do you know why those people are here? They've come to see Stanley get five hits today. Five hits!'"

—Jim Frey, Chicago Cubs manager,
remembering playing with Stan Musial

Jim Frey's story about Stan Musial illustrates the range of alternatives each of us has in our focus and self-talk in any situation. Musial had a positive expectation. He focused on the opportunity. "Do you know what this double header means today? It means Stanley *has a chance* to get *ten* hits!" Obviously, he was aware of the discomforts, but didn't deal with them like some of the others: ". . . somebody was *groaning* about *having* to play a doubleheader in the heat."

The heart and power of effective motivation is this positive expectation, "the passion for the possible."

When we are fully aware of the rewards and benefits of completing an assignment and when we believe we can do it, we are motivated. In my seminars I illustrate the power to determine our level of motivation by asking members of the group to give examples of difficult or distasteful experiences that they viewed as positive. Here are some responses:

1. A fifty-year-old insurance executive recalled that his summer job after graduating from high school was cleaning out horse stalls with his friend. As he told the story, his face lit up. He remembered being so dirty it didn't matter anymore, clowning around with his buddy, throwing horse chips, and generally feeling carefree.

2. Many people talk about the physical demands and rigors of Marine boot camp or late-summer football practice. The positives they mention are the feelings of accomplishment, digging deeper into their strengths, and camaraderie with others who are going through the experience.

3. A saleswoman described a recent snowstorm in Chicago, in which her whole family helped her teenage daughter meet her commitment to deliver newspapers. She remarked that the feeling of the family being together and working together to overcome obstacles was rare and wonderful.

4. Many women who went through natural childbirth said that in addition to the wonder of birth and delivering a healthy child, the pain, effort, and accomplishment of delivery gave them strong feelings of pride and confidence.

We've heard many other stories involving hard work, discipline, endurance, pain, and obstacles, and in each case the factor that made it positive was finding and focusing on the benefits or rewards. The people who gave these examples mentioned many benefits: feelings of accomplishment and competency, discovering more of your strengths and potential, teamwork and camaraderie, self-discipline, improvement, fun and spontaneity, and service.

The key question is, "Who determines my level of motivation for any given task?" The answer is, "I do. I can choose my focus ;and I can choose my self-talk and this strongly influences my motivation to complete a task." Let's look at the self-talk techniques for motivating ourselves positively and conquering procrastination.

SELF-TALK SECTION

Self-Talk #1
"I'm a person who is responsible, and I act in a timely manner to reach my goals and priorities."

Self-Talk #2

"This task is important and it's the kind I might procrastinate on or forget to do at all. I'm going to **do it now** and get it out of the way. It won't be hanging over my head and I'll be mentally free to concentrate on my other work or just relax."

Self-Talk #3

"This task needs to be done but I can't do it right now. I'm going to **schedule** a time when I know I'll be able to do it and stick to that schedule. If I don't there's a good chance I won't get to it. Now that I've scheduled it I can forget about it and concentrate on the job at hand."

Self-Talk #4

"When I complete this assignment I'm going to reward myself with my favorite . . . (food, item of clothing, TV show, movie, sports or leisure activity)

"I want to . . . (watch the football game, play golf, go shopping) at two. I'm NOT going to . . . (turn on the game, go golfing, go shopping) until I complete the work I need to do."

In the techniques described above, you reward yourself for doing jobs that you should do but tend to put off. They are very effective at increasing your motivation to start and complete the job. The key is to find appropriate rewards and apply them consistently.

Self-Talk #5

"This job looks so big that I'm avoiding doing anything. I'm going to break it down into smaller, manageable tasks and then get started on the first step."

Self-Talk #6

"I've been demotivating myself and avoiding this task. The hardest thing is to get started. I can make a commitment to working on this for ten minutes. After ten minutes I can stop and decide whether I want to continue."

Self-Talk #7

"I choose to do this because it is in my best interests, based on the current realities and my current goals. No one is forcing me to do this, and I don't 'have to' do it. I've assessed the consequences and the alternatives and on that basis I choose to do this.

"If I continue not to want to do this, I can explore different alternatives (delegate it, pay someone to do it, convince the person who assigned it to drop the assignment, work differently, change jobs, change companies)."

Self-Talk #8

"Every job has some elements that I will like and some that I won't like. There are certain 'givens' on this job. I know they will exist. They come with the territory.

"It's self-defeating to get myself upset over and over again when I know what's coming. I will accept these tasks and situations as part of an overall positive, desirable career, and remember that they play a role in my success and achievement."

Self-Talk #9

"When I have a task that is in my best interests to do, I motivate myself by focusing on all the benefits, rewards, and enjoyable aspects of completing it."

As salespeople we are aware of the need to be immersed in the benefits that our products and services provide. We "sell" by making customers aware of benefits that meet their needs or solve their problems. We can use this same process to "sell" ourselves on performing an activity.

If you need that extra push to overcome procrastination, it is very useful to complete a "benefits/rewards" list for that task. For example, if John decided that he needed to exercise regularly but continued to neglect it, he might brainstorm the following list.

BENEFITS/REWARDS: Regular Exercise

develop self-discipline

increase lung capacity

strengthen bones and muscles

endurance, stamina

more energy, zest

attractiveness

stress management

increase circulation, strengthen
  heart

joy of competition

develop potential

confidence, self-esteem

reduce blood pressure

control weight

can eat more without gaining
  weight

accomplishment

better mood, less depression

alone time (running)

break from work

fun (exercise with others)

make friends and business
  contacts

joy of movement, exertion

If John makes this list and then focuses on it regularly, he increases the probability that he will exercise. He has a much greater potential for overcoming procrastination than Joe, who is saying to himself, "Running is so boring! As soon as I start I can't wait for it to be over. I get so hot and sweaty and I hate those dogs barking at me. I know I should run; maybe I'll do it later when it cools off. Better yet, I'll start in the morning."

You can easily apply the same technique for any sales activity that is important to you but that you tend to avoid. Take prospecting by phone as an example.

BENEFITS/REWARDS: Prospecting by Phone

I can't lose what I don't have. Any prospect I gain is one more than I
  have now.

Phone calls lead to appointments; appointments lead to sales; sales
  lead to referrals.

I'm widening my base of contacts.

I'm learning about the marketplace.

I can improve my phone technique.

I can practice and experiment with new techniques.

If I learn to do the things other people don't like to do, I'll get ahead
  in selling.

My manager will appreciate my efforts.

The people I call need my products and services.

I can inform and help them.
I like meeting and talking to new people.
It will feel good to be disciplined enough to do this.
I'm going to reward myself when I finish.

Naturally, you can expand this list and tailor it to your own situation. The essential point is that you can "de-pattern" and reprogram yourself about any task. You can learn to like what you don't like. Whether the task is public speaking, writing thank-yous, paperwork, phone calling for prospects and referrals, reading, returning calls, writing proposals and reports, maintaining your business wardrobe, or following up, you can change your attitudes and begin to motivate yourself by positive expectancy, focusing on the rewards, benefits, and enjoyable aspects of the job.

Self-Motivation Activity

Practice this valuable technique now. Select an important task that you are avoiding or demotivating yourself about. Brainstorm a list of the benefits and rewards and the positive aspects of doing it. You may want to include these areas:

Advancement towards goals and rewards
Satisfaction of accomplishment
Self-discipline
New learning
Improving your skill or technique
Approval of others
Developing your potential
Any intrinsic enjoyment in the task
Ways to reward yourself for completion.

Put down all your positive reasons for taking action on this.

Transfer this list to a 3x5 card. Constant review will increase your tendency to complete this task.

Now let's pull together what you've learned about your procrastination patterns and the techniques that could help you eliminate them.

The Action Plan for Conquering Procrastination will help you decide which techniques you want to use for each specific activity that presents problems for you.

Exercise: Action Plan for Conquering Procrastination

Task/activity   Self-talk/techniques

1) Professional development

2) Maintenance

3) Responsibility to others

PART III

During The Sale

CHAPTER SEVEN

Managing Fear, Anger, and Discouragement

During the 1985 college football season,

number one-ranked Iowa played number

two-ranked Michigan. Iowa won, 12-10. A

week later, Michigan quarterback Jim

Harbaugh remarked, "It's hard to leave the

Iowa game behind, but we finally realized

that if we didn't, we were going to lose

again."

MENTAL PREPARATION AND positive self-motivation position us to create a productive sales contact. The true test of our self-mastery is how we manage our attitudes and emotions as we interact with prospects and customers.

Self-management skills during the sale are oriented toward two sets of objectives. The first goal is to continue the positive cycle we've begun by improving our inner environment. The second goal is to avoid negative patterns by noticing and correcting them quickly.

The Positive Cycle

The attitudes of confidence, friendliness, and service that we bring to a situation will often generate the responses we desire from our prospects. Trust and understanding develop and the sales process flows naturally to needs and solutions.

As Brian Adams says, "This client is my friend. He looks to me for guidance. This trust I truly appreciate. I return the compliment by giving my utmost attention to his needs. The transaction will be a fair and mutually beneficial one."

If the sales momentum is building, self-management requires us only to stay on track, focus on the customer, and concentrate at each stage of the sales process.

Here's some helpful self-talk:

Self-Talk #1.

Goals: Professional demeanor, confidence, calm.
"I concentrate on performing with a smooth, relaxed alertness."

Self-Talk #2.

Goals: Focus on customer, attitude of service.
"Whenever it is appropriate, I seek to ask the prospect or customer, 'Is there anything I can do to be more helpful in my dealings with you?' "

Self-Talk #3.

Goal: Concentration.
"My mind can focus effectively on one thing at a time. The best use of my time and energy is to concentrate on the details of the task at hand and take one step at a time."

Self-Talk #4.

Goal: Concentration, overcoming boredom and distraction, attitude of a learner.
"I overcome boredom because I concentrate on the details and nuances of each new situation. Because I'm always interested in learning, I'm always interested."

In *The Inner Game of Tennis*, Tim Gallwey says, "Concentration is the supreme art, because no art can be achieved without it, while with it, anything can be achieved."

The top sales performers have high "social IQs." They are alert and tune in accurately to the people they deal with. Their relaxed concentration throws light on the valuable details that make this situation unique. These salespeople take in essential information and adjust accordingly.

Concentration is the sales equivalent of keeping your eye on the ball. This alertness allows sales achievers to respond flexibly. They learn when to deviate from the normal pace or pattern, when to push, and when to back off. Their antennae are out, receiving signals and reacting appropriately.

Concentration is part intention and part practice. The good news is that every moment is an opportunity to practice the art of concentration. The self-talk above provides useful reminders.

Avoiding Negative Cycles

In this section we will learn how to avoid "making a problem out of a problem." Selling regularly involves problems and obstacles. Some are predictable, such as sales resistance, objections, complaints, "telephone tag," and slumps. Other problems are unpredictable, but they are equally a part of the sales experience. In Chapter 2 we read about the sudden appearance of a company lawyer (#1), spilled coffee (#4), a negative response to a presentation (#6), an abrasive secretary (#9), and an unexpected cancellation (#11). We can expect these problems, both predictable and unpredictable, to occur. We will label them "Problem #1."

What I refer to as Problem #2 is our upset and unhelpful reaction to Problem #1. Our reactions to sales problems include worry, anxiety, anger, irritability, discouragement, half-hearted effort, pushing too hard, and lack of concentration. These are normal, common responses, but they often make the situation worse and make it harder to achieve our objectives. (See Figure 8.)

The original problem has been compounded. When we are upset, we can't use our skills effectively or think clearly. Our

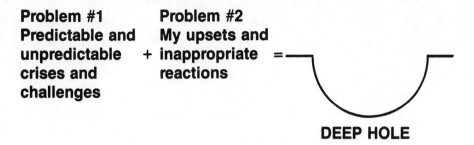

Problem #1
Predictable and
unpredictable
crises and
challenges

Problem #2
My upsets and
inappropriate
reactions

DEEP HOLE

Figure 8. Making a problem out of a problem.

emotional reaction may also affect the customer negatively. Rather than having a problem we can deal with, we may be on the road to the negative sales spiral that we described in Chapter 2. Psychologists call this pattern a "maladaptive response chain" of thoughts and actions.

All types of performances that are oriented towards results and deal with predictable and unexpected pressures are subject to these negative patterns. Musicians, artists, public speakers, athletes, test takers, and singers as well as salespeople, are all prone to Type 2 problems.

The consistently top performers not only develop their talents and master their "craft," but also learn to master themselves and deal positively and effectively with their Type 2 problems.

Problem Reactions

The most common problem reactions among salespeople can be categorized as:
- Fear reactions
- Anger reactions
- Discouragement

I will discuss each of these emotions, and will provide specific skills and guidelines for managing them. If any of these feelings are blocking your sales effectiveness, note the helpful self-talk and guidelines in each section.

Fortunately we do not need to, nor would we want to, eliminate all our upsets. Our goal is more control; more self-management, more mastery of our emotions while selling.

The road to improvement is paved with small successes. The road to perfection has many sinkholes. I advise you to focus on improvement, and strive for excellence. Leave perfection for the gurus.

Millions of salespeople have acquired productive attitudes through books, tapes, seminars, and good old trial-and-error selling experience. This book is designed to make the learning curve steeper and faster. Our motto is, "Improvement, not perfection." Our goals are to get upset less often, not to stay upset as long, and to be less upset if you are upset. These are realistic goals that you can achieve and build on. The confidence that develops from increased self-mastery promotes further improvements and successes.

IMPROVEMENT, NOT PERFECTION

		Frequency (how often)
Goals:	Reduce	Duration (how long)
		Intensity (how strong)
		of unwanted upsets

Fear Reactions

I feel well qualified to discuss the subject of worry because I studied for twenty years with one of the world's foremost experts on worry . . . my mother. At one time I thought I could show my mother that she had nothing to worry about. My brother and I were employed and married, and we each had two healthy children. When I mentioned these facts, she sighed and said, "Well, Marty, there is something I'm worried about . . . I'm worried that a cousin of mine is going to come to my funeral." You can see I've had a lot of opportunity to learn about worry!

Actually, we all know a lot about worry because it is universal.

My life has been a series of terrible misfortunes . . . most of which never happened.
—Mark Twain

Cowards die a thousand deaths; the brave man dies but once.
—Shakespeare, *Julius Caesar*

Both Twain and Shakespeare are pointing to a very important quality of fear. In fear, our bodies, minds, and nervous systems picture a painful event and then react almost as if it has happened. Like visualization, fear is a form of mental imagery in which we picture negative things occurring and tell ourselves how horrible they would be.

Chapter 2 provides several examples of fear inducing focus and self-talk:

#1. "This lawyer is going to kill the deal, just like the last one did."

#2. "This is really going to be embarrassing."

#4. "What a disaster! I'm going to look like a real slob at Dr. Johnson's office."

#6. "I'm bombing. I'm blowing the whole deal. . . . He'll never let me present a big deal again by myself."

#12. "I should call her but I hate to be pushy."

#13. "It's nerve-wracking waiting on such a big sale."

Worry and fear reactions can be useful if we use them as a signal to plan or take appropriate action. While we are selling, however, nervousness and anxiety usually work against us, and seem to have a life of their own.

As the greatest indicator of the potentially harmful effects of fear, the most repeated commandment in the Bible is, "Fear not—be not afraid."

In athletics and in selling, a key to peak performance is the management of tension and pressure. In selling specifically, fear reactions are damaging in the following ways:

Potentially Negative Effects of Fear

Focus. Fear is a negative visualization. In "dread rehearsal" we mentally go over negative outcomes and develop "tunnel vision."

Use of time and energy. Worry can rob us of valuable time and energy. While we are worrying we are not working on the problem or solutions. What is your *worry time* as compared to your *planning time* and your *solution time*?

Negative evaluations by prospects and customers. Customers and prospects are usually aware of nervousness or tension in a salesperson, as well as his general level of confidence and enthusiasm. Often it is difficult for them to develop trust and confidence in the salesperson if they perceive him or her as too tense or anxious.

Use of sales skills. Salespeople need to think clearly, communicate well, listen accurately and maintain good energy levels. Anxiety will often affect one or more of these areas so that just when the salesperson really needs his or her skills, they deteriorate.

Distraction and demotivation. Apprehensive feelings, tight muscles, restlessness and sometimes the desire to escape often distract a salesperson and can weaken his or her determination to persist.

Message. When we worry, we often are giving ourselves a subtle but penetrating message: "I won't do well. I won't be able to handle this." Often we picture ourselves embarrassed, rejected, or unable to cope. The overall message is one of weakness. When we worry we tend to ignore our strengths, our resourcefulness, our ability to bounce back and survive.

You can learn to manage your fears and anxieties while you are selling. You will learn self-talk responses and patterns that enable you to realize the following objectives:

Use fear and worry as a *signal*.

Quickly convert fear and worry to anticipation, concern, planning.

Develop a problem-solving approach, which reduces the time and energy that are wasted in fear and worry.

SELF-TALK SECTION

Self-Talk #1.
Goals: relaxation; enthusiasm; attitude of service; confidence.
"I focus on creating positive results in any situation. Problems give me an opportunity to learn, use my skills and demonstrate my commitment to the customer."

Self-Talk #2.
Goals: Reduce upsets; focus on improvement and learning.
"I'm disappointed with the results I'm getting so far. I'd better find out as much as I can about what is going wrong in this situation so I can improve it or at least get feedback to help me perform better in the future."

Self-Talk #3.
Goal: Short-circuit worry.
"Stop! Fear and worrying are a waste of my time and energy, and they block me from using my skills."

Before entering a sales situation, mentally review any problems and obstacles that could occur. Obtain all the information you can about the challenges of this situation. Plan and visualize how you would respond to each problem. The goal is to reduce worry through anticipation, planning, and preparation.

Self-Talk #4.
Goal: Confidence, reduced worry.
"I trust myself to acquire the knowledge and skills I need if this plan or approach does not lead to the results I want."

Self-Talk #5.
Goal: Focus on your ability to improve.
"I'm resourceful and I have the ability to bounce back. My trend is not my destiny because I can learn from my results and then change and adapt."

Self-Talk #6.
Goal: Reduce worry.
"My objectives in this situation are important. If I don't achieve them, I'll be disappointed and it will be inconvenient, but it will not be a catastrophe or a horrible event. By thinking about negative results as a catastrophe, I'm creating tension and fear that actually reduce my chance of success."

When you find yourself worrying, a useful sequence of self-talk is:
1. What is the worst thing that is likely to happen?
2. What would I do if that occurred?
3. What failures, setbacks, problems, and obstacles have I overcome or recovered from?

Self-Talk #7.
Goal: Remove pressure.
"I create pressure in any situation by what I focus on and what I say to myself. I can remove pressure by concentrating on doing the best job I can right now and learning all I can."

Self-Talk #8.
Goal: Reduce pressure.
"No one sale determines who I am, how good I am or how good I can be."

Fear and Worry Guidelines
1. Be aware of fear images and self-talk.
2. Change worry time into planning time.
3. Focus on learning and improvement.
4. Change catastrophes into inconveniences and disappointments.
5. Trust your strengths and resourcefulness.
6. You control the pressure valve.
7. Practice relaxation until you get good at it.

Exercise: Fear Reactions Inventory

List any sales situations where nervousness, fear, or worry block your actions of effectiveness in selling. Be as specific as you can. Don't leave out the things you avoid doing because of fears.

Write down some of your self-talk and describe your mental images in these situations.

Anger Reactions

The subject of anger generates a lot of heat, especially among experts who study it. There are countless, often opposing, points of view about how a person should handle angry feelings. You've heard everything from "suppress it" (count to ten) to "express it" (don't keep it bottled up).

I'm not going to try to resolve in a few pages a subject that has inspired thousands of books. Yet anger is an emotion that sales people need to discuss, understand, and manage. For most of us, frustrations and irritations are part of our daily sales experience. How we deal with them is a significant factor in our overall performance.

My approach is to examine both the positive and negative aspects of anger and to invite each salesperson to decide what is helping and what is hurting his or her efforts.

Potentially Useful Effects of Anger

Anger is a signal. It may convey important information for you about your stress level, sense of fairness, ego needs, or reactions to certain people. Anger can also be a signal to others about the depth of your feelings, and it can help them understand what is important to you.

Anger can motivate you and mobilize your energy and resources to get results.

The power of anger can intimidate other people. Some people rely on anger to get their way more often, although it is highly questionable how effective this technique is in sales situations.

Expressing anger can be a way of releasing various tensions that build up.

Potentially Negative Effects of Anger

Conflicts. Directing anger towards a prospect or customer usually works against establishing the trust and rapport necessary for the sales process. This is especially true early in the relationship. Sometimes it can feel good to "unload." Almost invariably, however, the sales person "wins the battle but loses the war" because the customer has the buying power. You can see the effect of unwanted conflicts in Case #1 (The Lawyer) on page 11 and Case #9 (The Bossy Secretary), on page 23.

Overall effect on the customer. Even if the salesperson is not angry directly at the customer, a generally angry mood usually has negative effects. Most customers like to do business with people who are pleasant and positive, and are not interested in the salesperson's problems. Consciously or unconsciously they withdraw from someone who is chronically angry or irritable. This is probably the case with John's customers in Case #8 because he is so negative (page 21).

Effects on sales skills. As with fear, anger often interferes with sales skills we need, particularly in difficult situations. When we are angry most of us don't listen as well, don't communicate as accurately (we may tend to make extreme or exaggerated statements), and focus on our own needs rather than on other people's. Thinking, decision making, and flexibility are also affected. This truth is expressed in a medieval Jewish saying: "Anger rusts the intellect."

In the introduction I defined sales performance as having skills and knowledge and being able to use them when it counts. Anger often prevents us from using our skills just when we need them the most. This is illustrated in Case #11, "The Canceled Order." Ron really needs to be at the top of his game, but he is starting to blow up (page 25).

Personal wear and tear. Being angry can often wear a person down both mentally and physically. For one thing, anger results in a massive physiological preparation for action. Drs. Meyer Friedman and Ray Rosenman, authors of *Type A Behavior and Your Heart*, describe the exact process:

> If you become intensely angered by some phenomenon, your hypothalamus will almost instantaneously send signals to all or almost all the nerve endings of your sympathetic nervous system (that portion of your nervous system not directly under your control), causing them to secrete relatively large amounts of epinephrine and norepinephrine . . . . In addition, this same fit of anger will probably also induce the hypothalamus to send additional messages to the pituitary

gland, the master of all endocrine glands, urging it to discharge some of its own exclusively manufactured hormones (such as growth hormone) and also to send out chemical signals to the adrenal, sex, and thyroid glands and the pancreas as well, so that they in turn may secrete excess amounts of their exclusively manufactured hormones.

Friedman and Rosenman go on to point out the dangers to our blood pressure and stress levels and coronary system if we chronically trigger this powerful reaction. For this reason it is important to use our anger more selectively; otherwise we may be punishing ourselves with the cumulative effects of being angry frequently.

At some point it is helpful to ask, "Am I doing something useful with this anger or am I mainly hurting myself?"

I will present self-talk and guidelines that can help you achieve more control over your anger. The goal is to reduce the times when being angry interferes with your sales performance. Total elimination of angry reactions is not achievable or desirable. The objectives are for you to review your sales experiences, decide if and when anger works against you, and then acquire the internal skills of managing this area of your emotional life.

SELF-TALK SECTION

Self-Talk #1.
Goal: Evaluating the effects of anger
Ask yourself these questions:
- Will being angry now help me reach my goals?
- Does it cause unproductive conflict?
- Will it detract from the use of my sales skills?
- Does it cause wear and tear on my system that limits my overall effectiveness?
- Is it hurting my relationship with this customer?

If you decide that your anger in a sales situation is working against your best interests, it is important to work immediately toward managing it. Different self-talk and skills will be useful, depending on why you are angry and how intense the anger is. The rest of this section will deal specifically with modifying anger. In Chapter 8, general self-management skills will be presented.

It is difficult to use good self-talk while you are upset, but there is an initial strategy for dealing with counterproductive upsets that many salespeople will find useful in a large number of situations. The keys to this approach are to convince yourself that the upset is working against you and to remind yourself that even though habit patterns are strong, you do have a choice.

Although we don't always realize it, we already employ this technique from time to time. We regularly adjust our emotional responses in light of our goals. Consider a married couple having a dispute in which they are both angry. The phone rings, and it's a mother-in-law, a minister, or someone else that they would prefer not to know they are having an argument. Their anger often disappears. We have more control over anger than we realize, and on occasion we exercise that control very successfully.

A manager used to get angry and criticize subordinates at meetings. After receiving feedback on the general ineffectiveness of this approach, he learned to wait until he was less angry and then deal with them one-on-one. Similarly, if we really understand and convince ourselves of the negative aspects of certain reactions in a situation, we are well along the road to making changes.

One change that is often available and useful is to acknowledge the upset but reduce the intensity.

Self-Talk #2.
Goal: Reduce the intensity of anger.
"I can achieve my goals in this situation with *firmness*. I don't have to be this angry. I can assert myself and be firm without being so angry or demanding."

Firmness is a very important concept and approach in selling and in other areas, because many of the situations we meet with anger can be handled as effectively—and often more effectively—with firmness. Firmness allows a salesperson to reduce counterproductive conflicts with a prospect or customer.

Self-Talk #3.

Goal: Reducing automatic anger that is triggered by problem people.

"I'm not a robot, I am free. No one can dictate how I will feel today. No one can push my buttons except me. I have a choice in how I'm going to react to this person."

Self-Talk #4.

Goal: Identifying positive alternatives to anger.
After an angry outburst that was unproductive:

"What result did I want? How could I have achieved it without being so angry?"

Self-Talk #5.

Goal: Focus on influencing people and improving working relationships.

"The only person I can ever control is myself. I can never control another person; I can only influence him. If I expect to be able to control him I'll probably be angry and frustrated. If I accept that I can influence his free choices I'll be calmer, learn more about him, and be much more effective."

The issue of control is closely related to our response of frustration and anger. Often we are prone to ways of thinking about control that make us more angry than is generally useful.

One counterproductive pattern is trying to control—and believing we should be able to control people we can't control, such as prospects, customers, secretaries, sales manager, or spouse.

When we believe we should be able to control people, we usually react with much more frustration and anger when they don't act the way we want. If we accept that people make free choices which we can influence, we are more likely to make the appropriate approach and less likely to react in an extreme way when their decisions disappoint us.

Self-Talk #6.

Goal: Reducing intensity of anger.

"I'm getting angry about a situation I can't control, and my anger will have no influence or effect. I'm wasting my time, energy, and resources, and I may carry my mood into my next situation and hurt my chances there."

This is a useful reminder. In many situations, our anger does no good and actually works against us. Traffic jams, plane delays, adverse weather conditions, and machinery breakdowns often trigger angry reactions that persist. A more useful approach is to move quickly from anger to acceptance of the reality to making productive use of your time and conserving your energy. Then, when you move into your next interaction, you will not bring along a negative mood or outlook.

Sandy Smith illustrates these ideas in his seminars by asking participants to name all the inanimate objects they get angry at. After some laughter the responses usually include the weather, cars, lawn mowers, golf balls, golf clubs, tennis racquets, alarm clocks, TVs, appliances, tires, and vending machines. Sandy then asks, "Do any of these things give a damn that you are angry?" Often this humorous question jolts the participants into examining just what they are accomplishing when they get angry at "things."

Self-Talk #7.
Goal: Reduced anger and annoyance.
"There are certain aspects of selling that I don't like or look forward to. These are *givens*. They are part of the territory and will be a regular part of my life. It's silly to get upset and annoyed over and over again when I know they are going to happen.

"My best approach is to change or improve the conditions I can, and accept that the other aspects are a given, a part of this career which I otherwise enjoy."

Often we will grow angry at sales resistance, objections, indecision, paperwork, unfriendly customers, rejection, changing market conditions, buyer's remorse, canceled orders. At some point, however, it is very useful to accept and expect these occurrences as part of a salesperson's life. This attitude will reduce how often and how intensely we get upset.

Self-Talk #8.

Goals: Developing "solution" consciousness; moving from upsets to action.

"When I get angry about not achieving the results I want in a situation, I move quickly 'from stewing to doing.' I try to obtain information that will lead to improvement now and in the future. I ask, 'What can I do to turn this situation around? Is there anything I can salvage from this situation? What can I learn from this situation? How can I prevent this from happening again?' "

It's unreasonable to expect that we will never be upset when things don't work out as we want. A key to success, however, is to use our upsets as a motivator and to move on to a productive phase of gathering information, learning, and acting.

We call this problem-solving approach "solution consciousness," and you can see this approach in many of the positive responses in the sales cases in Chapter 2. (It may be useful now to review some of the positive self-talk alternatives in those cases.)

Solution consciousness is the underpinning of top achievers because it helps us overcome worry, anger, discouragement, and distractions by focusing on learning and improving.

For an excellent example of the payoff of developing this approach and making it a habit, consider the experience of astronaut Jim Lovell on the Apollo 13 flight. An explosion occurred in mid-flight, and Captain Lovell's vital signs, as monitored in Houston, showed a definite fight-flight reaction peak. His nervous system recovered quickly, however, and his first words were calm and controlled: "Houston, I think we've got a problem."

Lovell had been so well trained to go from problem to problem solving that even though he had never been trained in that situation, he responded with a solution orientation, not panic or anger.

We can see another famous illustration of "solution consciousness" in the film classic *The Maltese Falcon*, although in this case the objectives are less than honorable.

As almost any movie lover will remember, Sydney Greenstreet plays Mr. Guttman, who has been searching for the falcon across several continents for seventeen years. Countless people have been murdered while trying to obtain the gold, jewel-encrusted statuette that was lacquered in black for deception. At the end of the movie Guttman finally has the falcon, and he feverishly rips off its packaging and begins to cut away the outside layer. As he cuts deeper and deeper he realizes that this falcon is a fake made of lead. His head jerks upward and his neck stiffens as if he has been dealt a sharp blow. Then his accomplices begin to make recriminations and place blame for the deception.

Guttman listens with a pained look, but within moments his face brightens. With a smile he says, "What are we to do, stay here and. rant and rave and call each other names? There's a falcon to be found. What is an investment of one more year, only 5 15/17% of what I've already invested in this pursuit? I suggest we make a hasty departure, considering our current circumstances."

Anger Guidelines
1. Ask yourself, "Is this helping me reach my goals?"
2. Reduce the intensity of the anger. Handle the situation with milder forms of anger. Appropriate firmness will achieve desired results in most sales contacts.
3. Remind yourself that you have a choice in how you are going to react to a person or an event.
4. Be an influencer, not a controller, and you will be less angry and more effective.
5. By being angry are you wasting time, energy, and resources and hurting your chances of success with your next customer?
6. Accept the givens of selling.
7. Develop solution consciousness and move quickly "from stewing to doing." Focus on improving, learning, salvaging, and preventing.

Anger Inventory

Write down specific ways in which being angry, frustrated, or irritable has negatively affected your sales performance. What is your self-talk in those situations?

Which self-talk and guidelines in this section will be most useful to you?

Discouragement

Dis-*courage*-ment is the lack of courage, hope, or a reason to persist. In sales situations discouragement comes in three forms:

1) discouragement about chances of success in a particular situation;

2) general doubts about the product and the marketplace;

3) discouragement about oneself and one's ability to sell.

Discouragement is always a danger when a salesperson, for a variety of reasons, doesn't initially achieve his or her sales objectives in a situation. His self-talk may include phrases like, "I can't . . . ," "they won't . . . ," "no one is . . . ," "I'll never . . . ," and other self-talk of discouragement.

Why is discouragement a very serious Type 2 problem, which makes the original problem so much worse?

I can illustrate the progressive negative effects of discouragement with a personal example from my childhood. During the singing rehearsal for my sixth-grade graduation, the music teacher stopped everyone and pointed to me in the back row. She said, "Young man, when we sing please move your lips only. Do not let any noise out."

You can safely assume that that one experience was enough to make me conclude, "I can't sing." Would you care to guess how much singing I did in public after that? Not much. How much better do you think I got, with no practice, no feedback and no coaching?

In other words, discouragement is a self-fulfilling prophecy. As Henry Ford said, "One person says 'I can do it,' the other person says 'I can't do it,' and they are both right."

Discouragement becomes reality for the same reasons I never got any better at singing. When we are discouraged many things change, and they are almost all bad. If we try at all, we don't make a full effort. Information seeking, experimenting and looking for alternatives grind to a halt. We stop looking for solutions; why invest energy and ego when "I know I can't do it"?

Psychologists have determined that *self-efficacy*; the belief that one's efforts will lead to results, is a crucial ingredient for success in any endeavor. Particularly in selling, the lack of self-efficacy—discouragement—is deadly.

Let's look at what a salesperson needs to achieve results:

1. Positive persistence. Persistence is the hallmark of top salespeople. They understand that the sales process involves overcoming sales resistance and objections, helping people make difficult decisions, dealing with buyer's remorse. When we become discouraged we tend to give up mentally. Even if we don't leave the situation we act half-heartedly, with no conviction or optimism. We have already accepted that we are not going to make the sale, so why put a lot of effort into it?

2. Mental toughness. Mental toughness includes the ability to perform at our top abilities regardless of conditions. Tim Gallwey defines it as never letting losing weaken our determination to win. Rejection and negative results are part of salespeople's day-to-day experience, and it is crucial to learn to respond in a constructive way.

3. The attitude of a learner. Earlier in the book I explained the power of the salesperson as a learner. A learner has a built-in antidote against discouragement by always focusing on improving and developing. That's exactly what learners do.

Tom Hopkins captures this idea when he advises about rejection, "You've already paid for the lesson, you might as well learn something from it."

SELF-TALK SECTION

Self-Talk #1.
Goal: Persistence.
"I focus on creating positive results in any situation. Problems are an opportunity for me to learn, use my skills and demonstrate my commitment to the customer."

Joe Gerard, the legendary car salesman and author of several sales best sellers, says that he can't wait for customers to have problems so that he can demonstrate true service and attention to their needs. Joe uses problems to turn customers into long-term clients.

Self-Talk #2.
Goal: Focus on learning and improvement.
"I'm disappointed with the results I'm getting so far. I'd better find out as much as I can about what is wrong so I can improve it or get feedback to help me perform better in the future."

Self-Talk #3.
Goal: Encouragement to move forward.
"I persist in a positive, flexible manner until I get things done."

Self-Talk #4.
Goal: Hope.
"My trend is not my destiny. I can learn from each situation and bounce back."

Self-Talk #5.
Goal: Encouragement.
"Other people sell this type of person and this type of account.

There is no such thing as a born salesperson. I can learn what I need to succeed if I'm willing to practice, study, and get feedback."

Self-Talk #6.
Goal: Increasing self-confidence; overcoming obstacles.
"This is a tough situation. I'll have to dig deeper. Now is the time really to use my professional skills. I welcome the chance to test myself."

Discouragement Inventory
Describe the customers, situations or conditions in your sales world that trigger discouragement for you. When do you give a half-hearted effort, or even avoid trying?

What is your self-talk when you are discouraged?

List the self-talk that would be most helpful for you to use when discouragement is blocking your effectiveness.

The next chapter will show how to use the helpful self-talk and mental skills we've learned to change how we feel and function while selling.

CHAPTER EIGHT

Self-Management Skills

The road to success is always under

construction.

—William Cook

SUCCESSFUL SELF-MANAGEMENT occurs when a sales-person becomes aware of negative thoughts or feelings and changes them quickly. This self-management sequence requires certain skills which you have been acquiring throughout this book. You've read many examples of sales people using these skills while they are face to face with prospects or customers. Here's another:

John G. is a 28-year-old car salesman at a BMW dealership in Dallas. He has learned to be comfortable with the luxury car buyer who tends to be confident, successful and assertive. On this particular day, however, John is showing cars to a very wealthy businessman and his wife, and he is not comfortable. John sees the man as arrogant and controlling. He says to him-self: "Who does this guy think he is? He acts like he knows more about cars than I do. Probably he bosses everybody around. Look at his wife; she's scared to death of him. He's one of these guys who wants the whole world to revolve around him."

As he starts to grow angry and tense, John notices his thoughts and feelings and alarm bells go off in his head. He says to himself, "I'm really building a case against this guy. If I keep it up I will either say something stupid or he will pick up my negative feelings. I'm killing my chances of making him my next buyer."

Having convinced himself that he needs to alter his self-talk quickly John continues, "I need to stop judging this man's character and start seeing him as a person buying a car, who has a right to buy the way he wants to. He's not insulting me directly. He just has a high opinion of his own knowledge, and isn't particularly interested in listening to me."

Then he develops a sales strategy. "I'd better back off, be respectful, and give him information when he asks for it. He's not the type of guy who wastes time so he probably is in here to buy. Now that I've changed my attitude I have a good chance to sell him."

Obviously John didn't learn to manage his emotions so well the first day on the job or after one seminar. Yet millions of salespeople use some version of these skills every day. Let's see how John did it.

1. He got upset. This is not desirable, but it is realistic. Good self-talk habits will prevent many upsets, but at times we will still experience inappropriate, unhelpful feelings.

2. He noticed his negative thoughts and feelings. This skill is absolutely crucial to effective self-management. A major lesson of this book is to help you start listening to yourself and to identify negative patterns quickly. When your unproductive self-talk hits you like a whiff of a bad odor, you are well on your way to making timely changes.

3. He confirmed that his upset would keep him from reaching his goals. Motivation to alter self-talk quickly comes from seeing clearly the negative impact of your current emotional state. John says, "I'm building a case. . . .; If I keep it up . . .; I'm killing my chances . . ."

4. He changed his self-talk, focus, and sales strategy. Note his new self-talk:

"I need to stop judging . . ."

". . . He has a right to buy the way he wants to . . ."

"He's not insulting me directly."

". . . he has a high opinion of his own knowledge . . ."

Also note his new strategy, focused on improvement and possibilities:

". . . be respectful and give him information when he asks for it."

". . . doesn't like to waste time . . . probably here to buy."

". . . I have a good chance to sell him."

This is the general model:

The Self-Management Sequence (SMS)

Step 1. Identify: "What am I thinking and feeling?"

Step 2. Evaluate: "How is this upset keeping me from reaching my goals?"

Step 3. Set goals: "How do I want to feel in this situation?"

Step 4. Replace: "What can I tell myself that is more realistic and helpful to change my focus and attitude?"

Step 5. Act on it: "My new strategy for this situation is . . ."

Step 1 is the awareness of what needs to change. Step 2 provides the motivation because the negative impact becomes clear. The third step is to focus on how you want to feel and point yourself in a specific positive direction. Then you need to change your self-talk. Eliminate the self-talk that is creating the unwanted feelings and replace it with helpful self-instructions. Finally, act on your new attitudes and feelings. Find the specific behaviors that are consistent with your new strategy for this sales relationship.

This sequence can take you where you need to be. The goal is not to make a problem out of a problem. Simply using the sequence will not make the original problem disappear, unless the only problem is your upset, but self-management does give you a decent chance of succeeding. By achieving the attitude and emotions you want, you remain in the batter's box. You may be fouling off pitches, but you haven't struck out. The opportunity for a sale is still alive.

The self-management sequence can become a performance habit. As a salesperson, you can convince yourself thoroughly that certain thoughts and feelings are undesirable. Their very appearance becomes a stimulus to use the sequence. Most of us tend to have repeated patterns. We can work out sequences to improve them, then practice and develop new response patterns.

While you are selling, self-management will become automatic and you can change negative situations in seconds. First, however, it is important to learn more about the steps and skills involved and then learn to apply them to your own sales contacts.

Inner Coaching Instructions

The total self-management sequence is a process of inner coaching. A key step is to discover the new self-talk and attitudes you want to be part of your inner vocabulary. I've provided sample self-talk in each chapter, and hope you will go further and develop some that fit you individually.

Once you have done this, you can shorten the whole sequence by using trigger words or phrases. These words need to be clear, direct, and meaningful to *you*. They serve as a stimulus and produce the desired results quickly.

Here are some examples of triggers that many salespeople use:

relax	influence
smooth	mentally tough
concentrate	improvement
service	stop
learner	control
only inconvenient	depattern
problem solver	I choose
firm	flexible

With repeated use these words become symbols of the attitudes, feelings, and actions you want to achieve. Saying them to yourself is an instant reminder and sets off a positive neuromuscular pattern.

Vigorous Disputing

Often, while trying to alter our self-talk and feelings, we become aware of a battle in our minds. These are persistent old reactions pitted against the new ways of responding.

Albert Ellis advises that in struggling with ingrained patterns you must be prepared to *dispute vigorously* the old way of responding.

You may have to say, "This is NOT a catastrophe! This is NOT horrible, humiliating, or the end of the world! It's inconvenient. I'm disappointed. Now I'm going to learn something and start again. So let's get going!"

Ellis is absolutely right. Our mental patterns are established. They will persist. If you assert new self-talk weakly and then fade away at any sign of resistance, you can pretty much expect to remain with the old feelings and patterns. Many people try alternative self-talk in that way and conclude that it is not effective. They will say, "I tried to tell myself not to be discouraged but the negative thoughts just continued. See, it just doesn't work."

This is why we need to practice and repeat new patterns until they are habitual. Even then there will be many times when you really have to do battle with your old self-talk.

Exercise: Designing Your
Self-Management Sequence (SMS)

Select a selling situation in which you were more nervous, angry, or discouraged than you would have liked to be. Choose one in which you can see how your feelings blocked your personal effectiveness.

Now complete this SMS chart.

1. How did my upset block me from reaching my goals?

2. What was my self-talk at the time?

(Write down the self-talk as exactly as possible. Don't censor it or clean it up. If you don't remember it, then ask yourself what self-talk was likely to create the feelings you had.)

3. How would I like to have reacted in that situation?

4. What self-talk would have been useful to reduce the negative feelings and to help me be more effective?

(Use self-talk you have learned in this book, or design your own.)

If you have completed this chart, you've planned a way to manage your emotions in that situation. The payoff comes from making the new response pattern a part of how you function.

Countering Cards

When you identify negative self-talk patterns that you use frequently, write them down on 3x5 cards. Write each pattern on the front of a card, and on the other side create helpful, alternative self-talk that would *counter* the negative pattern. Keep these cards handy and refer to them whenever you notice the unwanted self-talk blocking your effectiveness.

Example:

Side 1:

I hate to do this paperwork. What a drag! I shouldn't have to do all this. It's too much and it's boring.

Side 2:

This is obviously not my favorite part of this job, but it *is* part of it. Doing it in a timely way helps me and the company get paid and get feedback on the sales pace. I'm going to do it now, get it out of the way, and then watch that miniseries on TV.

Visualization and Mental Rehearsal

If you are in a game and ready to swing a racquet or a bat, you don't have much time to think about the perfect swing. Execution in these situations often depends on the hundreds or thousands of practice swings that you hope have established eye, hand, and muscle coordination.

A golf or tennis pro works on her swing until she creates a "groove," so that in the pressure of the game her mind and body respond automatically.

Salespeople can establish these same connections. In addition to using new mental skills in relating to actual customers, they can rehearse over and over again through visualization.

There are two basic ways of using self-management visualizations. One involves picturing yourself in difficult situations, using effective self talk and not getting upset. In the second approach, called the Stress Inoculation Method, you see yourself getting upset and then using appropriate self talk to calm down and perform successfully.

Preventing the Upset

Let us use the sales example that you just described in the SMS chart on page 125. Mentally rehearse handling the situation effectively in the following way:

1. Visualize the exact situation in detail up to the point where you are about to get upset.

2. Now envision yourself using the effective self-talk that you designed for this incident.

3. Repeat the self-talk with conviction until you can picture yourself in the situation, feeling the way you want to feel.

4. Now visualize your actions, speech, and body language reflecting how you feel inside. Note the positive effect on the customer.

5. Repeat the entire process until the mental pictures are clear and flow smoothly. The key is to do it until you really feel the appropriate emotion.

The Stress Inoculation Technique

Dr. Donald Meichenbaum has developed a remarkable technique that has proved in many instances to be the most effective approach to managing negative emotions. The goal is to prepare yourself for the fact that you may get upset and then to give yourself the skill and confidence to overcome it.

1. Visualize the exact situation in detail and see yourself having negative feelings. Experience them as you might in real life.

2. Now imagine yourself noticing the unwanted feelings and deciding to alter them.

3. Picture yourself using self-talk and internal skills to improve your feelings gradually. Then create a clear image of new attitudes and feelings becoming dominant in your mind.

4. Complete the visualization by seeing yourself perform competently and receiving a positive response from the customer.

5. Repeat the entire process until you become confident that *if you did get upset*, you would manage your feelings quickly and effectively.

These visualization techniques are very useful in preparing for new situations that might be difficult. I recommend strongly that if you have identified any negative emotional patterns, you design a self-management sequence to overcome them and then practice mentally using these techniques.

Acting on your new attitudes

Behavior reinforces belief. The best path to make new thinking part of your mental environment is to take action consistent with the new attitudes and beliefs.

A salesperson decides, for example, that she wants to change her attitude about failure and mistakes. In addition to using helpful self-talk about learning from mistakes, it is important for her to act on her new attitude. She might decide to try new sales approaches to see what she can learn. Instead of covering mistakes she could start to discuss them with other salespeople or with her manager. By setting up specific feedback systems she would show that she wants to learn and improve.

These changes in action will reinforce the changes in attitude, and fairly soon she really will have a new belief about failure and mistakes.

If you have decided to alter some attitudes, devote additional time to making your actions support the changes.

PART IV
After The Sale

CHAPTER NINE

The Self-Talk of Learning and Improvement

Don't refuse the lesson; you've already

paid for it.

—Tom Hopkins

JOHN MOORE, the sales manager of resort properties at Wayne Newton's Tamiment in the Pocono Mountains, relates this incident about salespeople's desire to learn. "I decided to provide a training seminar for my sales team, but I couldn't let everyone go through it at once. Since there were a number of people who were performing at a mediocre or marginal level, I decided to let these people attend the seminar first. My top performers would go through the training later. After I made this announcement I got two types of complaints. The poorer performers complained that they had to go to a seminar and the top salespeople complained because they couldn't get the training right now."

Moore's experience is repeated in some form on every sales force, every day. The best salespeople are *learners*; those salespeople who need the most improvement are often unwilling or unable to learn from their sales experiences and training. The "attitude of a learner," which we met first in Chapter Four, appears again in this discussion.

Alvin Toffler, the author of *Future Shock* and *The Third Wave*, advises us that the key skill of the future is *learning how to learn*. He suggests that most knowledge is continually becoming obsolete, but the person who knows how to learn will adapt and survive.

Talmudic rabbis, who spend their whole life in study and scholarship, bestow their highest praise on a colleague by saying, "He knows how to learn."

In sales, as in other endeavors, we sometimes place a great deal of emphasis on experience. "I've got twenty years of experience in sales," a salesman remarks. The question is, "Is it twenty years of experience or one year's experience twenty times?" The keys, then, are how much usable knowledge and skill we extract from our experiences and whether we continually seek out feedback and information.

We have already stressed the value of achieving the attitude of a learner. This attitude needs to be at the core of the salesperson's being because it is one of his main vehicles for defusing the disappointments, stresses, and rejections of selling. In fact, the self-talk and focus of a learner can often produce the *most* positive results when problems and failures occur.

Every salesperson will suffer disappointments and rejections. In a real sense, our sales careers depend on how we react to these events. There are three basic ways in which people react when they don't achieve the results they wanted or expected. These are shown in Figure 9, page 132.

I can illustrate the effect of these three reactions in an experience I had while working with Larry Wilson. Many salespeople know of Larry through his best seller *The One-Minute Salesperson* and his dynamic, hilarious motivational speeches.

In 1979 I developed some material and programs for Larry and for Wilson Learning Corporation, including a one-day event for a large West Coast bank. Larry always presented the material himself, but this time he said, "Marty, you designed a lot of this stuff, why don't you get up there with me?" At that point in my career I had taught small seminars of twenty people or less, and hadn't presented much to large groups. The bank expected five hundred employees to attend.

I accepted Larry's invitation, and we took turns presenting during the day. It was a long day. I bombed. I went "thud." My good friend was in the audience, and he couldn't even muster up a smile. At lunch I overheard a woman saying, "Gee, I hope that guy Wilson gets back on in the afternoon."

My techniques, which worked with twenty people, didn't work with five hundred. No one answered my questions. They weren't interested in my flip chart, and what the heck do you do with a microphone anyway?

Let's listen to the different self-talk I could have used in this situation.

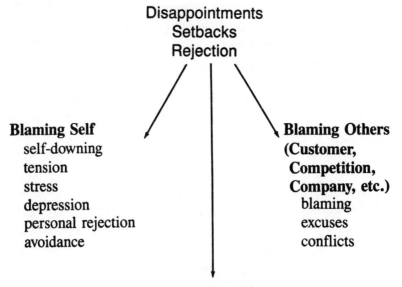

Figure 9. Reactions to disappointments in selling.

Blaming Myself

"What a disaster! This is the most embarrassing thing I've ever been through. I'm awful. What did I ever think I could do something like this? What a jerk to get on stage with Larry Wilson!"

How would I be feeling after saying this to myself? Did you hear me say anything that would help me improve? Actually all I did was increase the chances that I'd now avoid speaking to large groups.

This kind of self-talk is called "self-downing." Almost everyone does it. Most of us even have specific names we call ourselves when we miss a sale, miss a shot, or make mistakes. We rarely question this self-downing: does it do any good? Does it do any harm?

In seminars I ask people to write down the bad names they call themselves and then repeat them to another participant. Usually they laugh and cry at the same time. The names we call ourselves can hurt, and often, as in my example, there is very little focus on improvement.

Blaming Others

"What a bunch of losers! I'm trying to give them some ideas that could help them and they aren't even interested. They would rather have Larry come up and entertain them than really learn something. It's stupid even to try one of these programs where the president of the bank tells them to show up. They don't even want to be here. It's a waste of my time and energy."

That got me off the hook, didn't it? It's not hard to find excuses and people to blame. We've probably all heard some strange excuses and used some ourselves. But what happens if blaming others for poor performance becomes a habit? I might feel better by using this self-talk, but the odds are very low that I would learn anything that I need to learn. When I blame other people, I'm not looking at myself as part of the problem or part of the solution.

Calm Self-Critique

"I'm really disappointed with how I did today. I misjudged so many things about working with a large audience, and the way I performed is unacceptable.

"I realize this is the first time I've done this, so I need to put my results in perspective. I know I have some strengths to build on. I'm articulate, I care about people, and I've got a good grasp of the material.

"Now I need to improve. I can see some things to do differently but I'd better ask Larry and some people from the bank to give me specific feedback."

This approach is really a skill. It is an extremely valuable, lifelong skill that is the core of the attitude of a learner. Notice that in this self-talk I expressed disappointment but I didn't destroy myself. I focused specifically on what I did wrong but I put my performance in an overall perspective.

By reminding myself of my strengths, I encourage myself to begin to focus on improvement. I can't improve without the guidance of feedback.

Individuals who practice calm self-critique achieve rapid progress. Their greatest edge is that while most people avoid or reject feedback, these people seek it actively and monitor their performance regularly.

In the actual situation I reacted in all three ways but settled down to the attitude of a learner (after all, I was teaching this attitude). Larry and my friend in the audience gave me feedback about ten things I should do differently. I listened and changed and worked with Larry successfully many times after that. I'm grateful for the opportunity and the honest feedback he gave me.

The Learner: "Protection vs. Correction"

Stewart Emery explains that each of us faces moments of truth when we perform. We can choose "protection" or "correction."

He uses these terms to distinguish between those who want to improve and thus open themselves up for feedback ("correction") and those who try to "protect" themselves by covering and hiding their weaknesses and areas that they need to improve.

Often, when I'm called in to conduct training in organizations, I ask, "What do you do around here when you make mistakes?" Too often the reply is, "Don't tell anybody."

This attitude that mistakes are terrible and embarrassing can often lead us to hide them rather than correct them and improve our performance.

In sales seminars, when dealing with specific techniques like handling objections, I often ask salespeople to tell me what they have been saying currently. One day a saleswoman gave a response that shocked me. I asked, "Have you had much success when you say that?" She replied, "No, I haven't made a sale in six months when that objection came up. I've been hoping that people won't bring it up."

This woman went on to become an excellent salesperson, but she had to overcome the need for "protection." As she revealed what she had been doing, she saw how harmful it was and became determined to seek information and input from others when she needed it.

We can see how this need for "protection" hurts our development if we look at a tennis player who runs around her backhand and tries to use a forehand instead. She may be able to win some matches, depending on her other abilities, but there will always be a limit to her development because she won't improve her backhand.

At higher levels of play she will encounter players who were willing to hit their backhands, make mistakes, lose matches, but eventually improve. The learner also wants to win. The learner has a unique kind of drive for excellence that is achieved through trying, risking, trying again, and a willingness to seek and receive feedback.

Above all people, the learner realizes that accurate feedback from all sources is the key to improvement. Mere practice and repetition will not necessarily help us because we can practice the wrong things. The salesperson with the learner's attitude realizes that the decisions of the prospect or customer are feedback about him, his product, and the marketplace. In addition he puts himself in a position to obtain feedback from other salespeople and sales managers. Later in this chapter we will explore the various ways in which salespeople can receive this valuable feedback.

A baby learning how to walk demonstrates the attitude of a learner in the clearest way. When the baby falls down, its brain, nervous system, and muscles learn. The baby doesn't count the mistakes because its focus is on the goal—walking—and that's what it eventually achieves.

Thank goodness a baby doesn't have some of our self-talk; otherwise it would never learn to walk.

"Oh no, I fell down again; that's the tenth time today. I'm terrible at this. I'll never learn to walk."

"I'm a year old now and I still can't walk. My sister walked when she was ten months old; what's wrong with me?"

Here is the self-talk that can help you extract the most learning from your sales experiences.

SELF-TALK SECTION

Self-Talk #1.
Goal: Useful information.
"There are experts and professionals in my field who will help me learn, improve, and excel. They will respond to my sincere, thought-out questions and concerns."

Self-Talk #2.
Goal: Calm attitude; focusing on improvement.
"I can calmly review and critique my performance and then make improvements without calling myself names or blaming my performance on someone else."

Self-Talk #3.
Goals: Openness to feedback; setting up feedback systems.
"I'm more interested in correction than protection. I know I can learn and improve whenever I make mistakes or don't achieve the results I want. I systematically obtain feedback from my

managers, peers, customers, and prospects and by monitoring my own performance."

Sources of Feedback

Depending upon their individual circumstances, salespeople can obtain valuable feedback from a variety of sources. Here is a partial list:

Asking customers and prospects directly

Prospect and customer questionnaires and surveys

Observation by peers

Postsale review with manager

Making tape of simulated presentations

Role playing and simulations

Observing self in mirror while practicing

Videotape of practice presentations or other aspects of the sales process

Monitoring systems for keeping track of prospecting and other sales activities

Monitoring success and failure patterns

The following guidelines are useful for encouraging people to give you feedback and for extracting the most useful information from the feedback you receive.

Guidelines for Receiving Criticism or Feedback

Make eye contact.

Clarify the feedback until you are receiving information about specific behaviors that you have a choice about.

Find out how the other person thinks you could improve.

Let him or her know you have heard their feedback.

Thank him.

Explain how it may influence your future actions.

Self-Talk #4.

Goals: Learning from negative reactions; reducing stress.

"I am always alert to people I have a strong negative reaction to and people who have a strong negative reaction to me. These people can be my very important teachers. In these situations, I ask myself: 'What was my self-talk?' 'Is there anything useful I can learn about myself?' "

Self-Talk #5.
Goals: Reducing upsets; focusing on learning and improvement.
Ask solution-consciousness questions: "What can I learn?" "Is there anything I can salvage?" "What can I do to prevent this from happening in the future?"

Self-Talk #6.
Goal: Catching yourself doing something right.
"What did I do well in this interaction that I want to remember to keep doing?"

Feedback and focus on what you are doing right are more valuable in many ways than negative feedback. If you discover what works, identify it and make it part of your regular sales approach. All too often the boast, "I've forgotten more about that than you'll ever know," may be true but regrettable.

Countless times in seminars I've heard salespeople remark, "You know, I used to do that and it worked." Perhaps you've had the same reaction while reading some of the principles and techniques in this book.

For this reason it's crucial to take some time after each interaction, sale or no sale, and identify what you liked about what you did.

Self-Talk #7.
Goal: Acquiring information about where you need to improve.
"What errors did I make? What would I do differently?"

Self-Talk #8.
Goal: Identifying tendencies toward errors.
"Was this a one-time error or do I have a tendency to make these mistakes?"

Obviously, our real Achilles heel is the pattern of mistakes or incorrect strategy that we repeat. It is vital to identify these tendencies as soon as possible, because that's where we need to focus our efforts.

If we critique each performance, even for a few minutes, we will be able to spot problem areas.

Self-Talk #9.
Goals: Optimism; encouragement.
"I'm alert to learning every day and this builds in me a sense of optimism, energy, and a successful future."

Self-Talk #10.
Goals: Calm self-critique, visualizing success.
Visualization technique: Mentally picture yourself making a sales mistake and calmly critiquing your behavior. Concentrate on maintaining a calm attitude and genuine concern for improvement. Then mentally replay the sales situation, but this time picture yourself as having made the necessary corrections and performing without mistakes.

This exercise goes right to the heart of the attitude of a learner. It is usually important to rehearse this calm self-critique mentally, because it is unusual for most of us to be highly motivated to change and yet not be too upset with ourselves.

The importance of admitting mistakes and taking responsibility for results is illustrated vividly in an anecdote related by Bill Byrne, chairman of the Byrne Corporation. During his National Football League career, Byrne played under head coach Blanton Collier. After missing a tackle in practice, he was approached by Collier, who asked what happened. Byrne started to give an excuse and blame someone else for missing an assignment. While he was talking, Collier turned his back and began to walk off the practice field. Byrne yelled, "Coach, where are you going? It's the middle of practice!" Collier replied, "What's the sense in staying here when I can't coach you?"

Byrne immediately got the message and took responsibility for his error on the play. Collier replied, "Fine, now I can coach you."

Obviously, Blanton Collier was acutely aware that blaming and excuses, although sometimes partially justified, are a tremendous block to improving. The blame or excuse allows us to not look at what we need to do differently.

I have the pleasure of working with Bill Byrne today, and he uses the attitude of a learner and solution consciousness regularly and effectively in a high-stakes environment.

Self-Talk #11.
Goal: Personal responsibility for results.
"I take full responsibility for my thoughts, my feelings, and my actions. I'm accountable for the results I achieve."

Self-Talk #12.
Goal: Preserving and supporting effective attitudes and mental skills.
"My time and energy are precious. I choose to surround myself with positive associates who are focused on possibilities, learning, improving, and taking responsibility for results. I guard my mental life against negative influences."

Which skills and self-talk in this chapter would be most helpful to you?

THE SALES CHALLENGE

For more than twenty years I have been fascinated by the process of human beings growing and developing their potential. My personal pursuits have included training in a Japanese monastery, clinical psychology, commodities trading, long-distance running, racquetball, taking care of babies, organizational consulting and for the past ten years, sales and sales training.

I have tried to learn about personal excellence from everyone I've observed or talked with, from professional athletes to professional poker players. Sales professionals have taught me about courage and commitment. As I review my ten years as a salesman I realize that selling has been an important pathway to personal development as well as a way to support my family and spread my ideas.

I hope this book will help you develop your "inner coach" and that this coach will help you achieve, excel, and realize your potentialities.

You are to be admired for being willing to "put yourself on the line," learn about yourself and change old habits. May your persistence bring rewards for you, your company, and your customers.

Marty Seldman
Granville, Ohio

APPENDIX 1

The Winning Edge: Test and Review

In the next section you will be invited to complete a personal Sales Performance Profile, which will help you plan and monitor your progress. Before you develop this profile it may be useful to review the skills and attitudes that have been presented and to test your ability to identify them.

Figure 10 is a list of the key performance attitudes and skills you have learned. Test your knowledge by reviewing the performance of Susan T.—Condominium Sales (Introduction, pages iii-v) and the –positive self-talk– examples in each of the twelve cases (Chapter 2). In the space provided, write down any helpful skill or attitude that you recognize in these performances.

After you have completed the test, you can check your results against the suggested answers provided on pages 147-150.

Attitudes	Skills
Attitude of a learner	Professional Sales Preparation
Solution consciousness	Concentration
Attitude of service	Mental rehearsal and visualization
Focus on the customer	Use of cards and audiotapes
"I am sold myself."	Self-management sequence and skills
The will to win	Relaxation
"Mistakes are lessons."	Positive self-motivation
Inconvenience vs. catastrophe	Stress inoculation
Persistence	Calm self-critique
Gratitude	Feedback systems
	Inner coaching
	Self-recognition and reinforcement

Figure 10. Performance attitudes and skills.

Review Test

Susan T.—Condominium Sales
Attitudes:

Skills:

In each of the twelve case studies analyze the positive self-talk alternative, which appears last. In Case #1, for example, analyze the self-talk of Salesman B.
Case 1: Corporate Insurance Sales
Attitudes:

Skills:

Case 2: The Stockbroker and the Entrepreneur
Attitudes:

Skills:

Case 3: Prospecting by Telephone
Attitudes:

Skills:

Case 4: The Bad Start
Attitudes:

Skills:

Case 5: The Pessimistic Saleswoman
Attitudes:

Skills:

Case 6: Problems During the Sales Presentation
Attitudes:

Skills:

Case 7: After Making the Sale
Attitudes:

Skills:

Case 8: After Losing the Sale
Attitudes:

Skills:

Case 9: The Bossy Secretary
Attitudes:

Skills:

Case 10: The "Typical" Owners
Attitudes:

Skills:

Case 11: The Canceled Order
Attitudes:

Skills:

Case 12: The Distracted Car Salesman
Attitudes:

Skills:

Suggested Answers

Susan T.—Condominium Sales

Attitudes:
Solution consciousness
"I am sold myself."
Focus on the customer
The will to win
Attitude of a learner
Inconvenience
Persistence

Skills:
Professional sales preparation
Positive self-motivation
Self-management sequence (worry)
Use of cards and tapes
Mental rehearsal and visualization
Stress inoculation
Calm self-critique

Case 1: Corporate Insurance Sales
Attitudes:
"I am sold myself."
Attitude of service
Focus on the customer
Inconvenience

Skills:
Inner coaching
Relaxation
Concentration
Self-management skills (anger, discouragement)

Case 2: The Stockbroker and the Entrepreneur
Attitudes:
Focus on the customer
"I am sold myself."
Attitude of service

Skills:
Professional sales preparation
Positive self-motivation

Case 3: Prospecting by Telephone
Attitudes:
Gratitude
The will to win
Persistence

Skills:
Positive self-motivation
Relaxation

Case 4: The Bad Start
Attitudes:
Inconvenience
Solution consciousness
Mistakes are lessons

Skills:
Self-management skills (worry)
Positive self-motivation

Case 5: The Pessimistic Saleswoman
Attitudes:
"I am sold myself."
Solution consciousness
The will to win
Attitude of a learner

Skills:
Positive self-motivation
Self-management skills (discouragement)

Case 6: Problems During the Sales Presentation
Attitudes:
Attitude of a learner
Inconvenience
Solution consciousness
Mistakes are lessons

Skills:
Self-management sequence (fear, discouragement)
Feedback systems
Calm self-critique
Relaxation
Concentration

Case 7: After Making the Sale
Attitudes:
Attitude of a learner

Skills:
Self-reinforcement
Calm self-critique

Case 8: After Losing the Sale
Attitudes:
Attitude of a learner
Solution consciousness
Persistence

Skills:
Self-management skills (discouragement)
Feedback systems
Calm self-critique

Case 9: The Bossy Secretary
Attitudes:
Solution consciousness
Focus on customer
Attitude of service
Attitude of a learner
Inconvenience

Skills:
Self-management skills (anger)

Case 10: The "Typical" Owners
Attitudes:
Focus on Customer
Attitude of service
Attitude of a learner

Skills:
Professional sales preparation

Case 11: The Canceled Order
Attitudes:
Solution consciousness
Attitude of a learner

Skills:
Self-management skills (anger)
Positive self-motivation

Case 12: The Distracted Car Salesman
Attitudes:
Focus on the customer

Skills:
Concentration
Self-management skills
Professional sales preparation

The Sales Performance Profile

It has been remarked that a professional is someone who is good at what he or she does; knows he is good and knows why he is good. I would add another important dimension: that the professional also knows when he is *not* good and why.

I would like to help you create your own Sales Performance Profile, which will give you an overview of what helps you or hurts you in selling. It will help you focus on creating the conditions you need to perform at the top of your game, and will also provide a way for you to monitor your performance and give yourself feedback.

There are three steps to creating this profile.

1. Peak Selling Conditions

Visualize in detail three sales situations in which you feel you have performed at the best of your abilities. Identify the attitudes, feelings, and behaviors that you feel contribute to your effectiveness.

Attitudes

Feelings

Behaviors

2. New Self-Talk and Internal Skills

In this book you have been exposed to many examples of self-talk, mental techniques, and internal skills that you may want to make part of your peak selling conditions. Add these to your performance profile.

New attitudes and self-talk

New techniques and skills

Specific action plans to acquire new skills and habits (cards, tapes, mental rehearsal, reviewing book, feedback, group discussion)

3. Nonproductive Patterns

You have also learned about nonproductive self-talk patterns and emotional responses that hurt sales performance. One of the quickest ways to improve your effectiveness is to identify and change these patterns, particularly if there are one or two that trip you up regularly. Try to focus on habits that work against you both in the short term and in the long run.

Harmful habits and patterns

4. Monitoring Systems

We suggest that you make copies of your profile, and rate your performance on a sales call at least twice a week. A scale of 1 to 5 is useful, with 1 being poor and 5 excellent. Focus on each of the three components.

Are you doing the things you know help you produce?

Are you adding desired self-talk and skills to your repertoire?

Are you reducing the frequency, duration, and intensity of your negative patterns?

Training Guidelines
for Sales Managers

This book and related training products can be used by sales managers and executives in a variety of ways to increase the effectiveness of their sales teams.

1. Self-Study, Self-Reinforcement

The format includes many case studies, activities, exercises, and skill practices. It is designed to make salespeople aware of where they need to improve, and then shows them how to do it.

Individuals can easily acquire these insights and skills through self-study, but the new mental habits and sales skills they choose to develop need to be repeated and reinforced. To support these efforts, a self-talk card system and cassette tapes are available (see page 160).

2. Sales Team Meetings

The material in each chapter can be covered in two or three one-hour meetings; discussing the ideas and skills in a group maximizes learning for everyone. Most managers have found it useful to ask their salespeople to discuss the problems and successes related to the situations described in a chapter.

Follow-up sessions are useful to review the use of skills and techniques and to build on improvements. The overall objective is to enable salespeople to continue on a path to positive mental and emotional self-management. It is not crucial that each individual use the skills in the same way.

3. Coaching Individuals

If a salesperson completes the case study exercises and personal activities in the book, he or she will gain useful insight into some areas where improvement is needed to develop sales talent more fully. To help in this process I have included a test and review (Appendix 1) and a Sales Performance Profile (Appendix 2), which will provide an overview of how the salesperson functions and an action plan to create consistently favorable selling conditions.

This profile, combined with any other awareness the salesperson is willing to use and share, can provide an excellent basis for coaching and career development talks.

If a sales manager discusses the profile with each member of the sales team, a team profile will emerge. A number of sales managers have used this information as a basis for assessing specific training needs.

Best wishes for success in helping your sales team develop "The Winning Edge."

REFERENCES AND RECOMMENDED READINGS

Adams, Brian, *Sales Cybernetics*. North Hollywood, CA: Wilshire Book Co., 1985.

Alessandra, Anthony J., and **Wexler, Phillip S.,** *Non-Manipulative Selling*. Reston, VA: Reston Publishing Co., 1979.

Bliss, Edwin C., *Doing It Now*. New York: Charles Scribner's Sons, 1983.

Butler, Pamela E., *Talking To Yourself*. Briarcliff Manor, NY: Scarborough House, Stein and Day, 1981.

DeBono, Edward, *New Think*. New York: Basic Books, 1967.

Ellis, Albert, *Executive Leadership, A Rational Approach*. New York: Citadel Press, 1972.

Ellis, Albert, and **Harper, Robert,** *A New Guide to Rational Living*. Hollywood, CA: Wilshire Book Co., 1977.

Ellis, Albert, and **Kraus, William,** *Overcoming Procrastination*. New York: Institute for Rational Living, 1977.

Gallwey, W. Timothy, *The Inner Game of Tennis*. New York: Random House, 1974.

Garfield, Charles and **Bennett, Hal Z.,** *Peak Performance*. Los Angeles: Jeremy P. Tarcher, Inc., 1984.

Hill, Napoleon, *Think and Grow Rich*. Brooklyn, NY: Fawcett Crest Books, 1960.

Hopkins, Tom, *How to Master the Art of Selling*. New York: Warner Books, 1982.

Hopkins, Tom, *The Official Guide to Success*. New York: Warner Books, 1982.

Johnson, Spencer, M.D., and **Wilson, Larry,** *The One-Minute Sales Person*. New York: William Morrow & Co., Inc., 1984.

Kennedy, Danielle, *Super Natural Selling*. San Clemente, CA: Craig Publications, 1984.

Lewis, Robert, *Taking Chances*. Boston: Houghton Mifflin Co., 1979.

Loehr, James E., *Athletic Excellence: Mental Toughness Training for Sports*. Denver, CO: Forum Publishing Co., 1982.

Marc, Robert, *Managing Conflict from the Inside Out*. San Diego, CA: Learning Concepts, University Associates, 1982.

Maultsby, Maxie C., Jr. *Help Yourself to Happiness Through Rational Self-Counseling*. New York: Institute for Rational Living, 1975.

Maultsby, Maxie C., Jr., and Hendricks, Allie, *You and Your Emotions*. Lexington, KY: University of Kentucky Medical Center, 1974.

Meichenbaum, Donald, *Cognitive-Behavior Modification*. New York: Plenum Press, 1977.

Moorman, Chick, *Talk Sense to Yourself: The Language of Personal Power*. Portage, MI: Personal Power Press, 1985.

Stern, Frances Meritt, and Zemke, Ron, *Stressless Selling*. Englewood Cliffs, NJ: Prentice-Hall, 1981.

Timmerman, Tim, and Blecha, Diane, *Modern Stress: The Needless Killer*. Dubuque, IA: Kendall Hunt Publishing Co., 1982.

Tutko, Thomas, and Tosi, Umberto, *Sports Psyching*. Los Angeles: J.P. Tarcher, Inc., 1979.

FURTHER INFORMATION & SERVICES

Dr. Marty Seldman received his Ph.D. in clinical psychology from Temple University in 1971. He is an international consultant specializing in sales and management training, executive coaching and organizational development and is currently CEO of Ridge Assoc., a training and consulting company in Cazenovia, New York. He offers a variety of services and audio/video products related to the principles and ideas discussed in this book.

To find out more contact:

Dr. Marty Seldman
P.O. Box 431
Granville, Ohio 43023
(614) 587-2467